The Missouri Review

Volume XIV Number 3   1991

University of Missouri-Columbia

EDITOR

Speer Morgan

MANAGING EDITOR

Greg Michalson

ASSOCIATE EDITORS

William Peden, Jo Sapp, Evelyn Somers

ADMINISTRATIVE ASSISTANT

Dedra Veach

SENIOR ADVISORS

Jim Jackson, Ken Love, Christian Michener

ADVISORS

Ryan Gilbert, Liz Oyen, Brenda Squires, Jeff Thomson

INTERNS

Lisa Copenhaver, Sheila Curry, Grant Davis, Danica MacDonald,
Julie Silvestri, Kris Somerville, Angela Spicer

The Missouri Review is published by the College of Arts & Science of the University of Missouri-Columbia, with private contributions and assistance from the Missouri Arts Council and the National Endowment for the Arts.

The diary of Peter Pitchlynn is by arrangement with the Western History Collection of the University of Oklahoma Library.

The photograph of Peter Pitchlynn courtesy of the Library of Congress.

Cartoons in this issue by Brad Veley.

The editors invite submissions of poetry, fiction, and essays of a general literary interest with a distinctly contemporary orientation. Manuscripts will not be returned unless accompanied by a stamped, self-addressed envelope. Please address all correspondence to The Editors, *The Missouri Review*, 1507 Hillcrest Hall, University of Missouri, Columbia, Missouri 65211.

SUBSCRIPTIONS

1 year (3 issues), $15.00
2 years (6 issues), $27.00
3 years (9 issues), $36.00

Copyright © 1991 by The Curators of the University of Missouri

ISSN 0191 1961   **ISBN** 1-879758-02-4

Typesetting by HiTec Typeset, Columbia, MO.
Printed by Thomson-Shore, Dexter, MI.

CONTENTS

1991

FICTION

INTERVIEW

FOUND TEXT SERIES–Peter Pitchlynn

POETRY

ESSAYS

"You don´t mind if we sing another little song
about _me_, do you?"

Foreword

Several of the pieces in this offering concern children and the relations between children and parents. Will Baker's "Gorepac" is a spine-tingling allegory of a family living either now or in the near-future, I shudder to think which. C. W. Smith weaves an elegant saga of discord and reconciliation in "A Letter from the Horse Latitudes," and Tricia Tunstall tells of "The Taming of Monsters" shared by mother and son. Kim Edwards' wonderfully real teenagers in "No Permanent Bad Thing" teach us a thing or two about what young lovers really want, while Norman Lavers' "Telegraph Relay Station" operator tries to create and maintain romances against all odds.

The three featured poets in this issue often write about history and place, as well as about family. Walter McDonald's lively, often playful poems take as their starting point people and landscape, and Liz Rosenberg is inspired by the small gestures of children and friends. The vistas in Bruce Bond's landscapes are more dreamlike, with larger sweeps of the canvas.

I love the personal memoir "Shared Voices" by novelist Mary Lee Settle. It begins by mentioning that she grew up in an era when parents found children a chore, hopefully to be taken care of by someone else. Because Settle was uninterested or inept at most of the preferred after-school activities, she ended up taking "elocution" from an intimidating and somewhat spooky fellow. He would give her an unexpected, priceless gift—read on!

This issue's "History as Literature" manuscript provides a look at the forced removal of Native Americans from their homelands.

Expulsion and relocation of Native Americans in this country was a consistent governmental policy executed throughout most of the nineteenth century. The protagonists of removal, both white and Indian, portrayed it to be a kind of universal solution for tribal problems. The cost of this policy was thousands of lives. By the 1870s, when the Indian Territory (later Oklahoma) was being overrun by whites, a growing body of Indian "philanthopists," "experts," government officials, and some tribal members began to push the next grand solution: the policy of severality, which would abolish tribes as landholding institutions and allot land to individuals.

White philanthropists passionately believed that allotment was the last chance to salvage some justice for Indians. In their minds, the woes of the heathens derived from their habits of slothfulness, profligacy, sociability, and communism. Ending communal land ownership was seen as the key to fixing everything else. It was the magic bullet for the "Indian problem." Government panaceas have a way of turning into their own opposites, and severality was exactly that—the antithesis of the previous grand solution. Instead of creating safe "reserves" of tribal land, they would abolish the tribes and parcel out their land. The Indian governments, particularly the Seminole, Cherokee, and Choctaw, fiercely resisted allotment, as they had resisted removal sixty years before, and again they lost.

Because of the strength of their resistance, the original Dawes Act excluded the Five Civilized Tribes from allotment, but a few years later the Dawes Commission was set up specifically to enforce allotment among these tribes. The Dawes Commission employed five hundred bureaucrats and took twelve years, but by the turn of the century it had succeeded in breaking down tribal resistance, determined the tribal rolls, and taken possession of the largest estate known in western history, 31,000 square miles of Indian lands. A fraction of this land was allotted to tribal members and the rest was disposed of in various ways. Native Americans were now thrown into the rough and tumble of the great American real estate game. In effect, what remained of their lands was put into the hands of individuals many of whom were poor and could ill afford to hold on.

Peter Pitchlynn was a mixed-blood Choctaw whose life would span both eras; born and raised in the Mississippi homelands, influential throughout his life, he first became involved in tribal affairs at the beginning of the removal period. Pitchlynn would live to see the craze for allotment take hold, although he had died before the tribe finally gave up resistance, in 1898.

As a young man, Peter Pitchlynn went on a journey of exploration, set up in 1828 by federal negotiators, to the land which had been designated to be the Indian Territory. He kept a diary of this journey, and continued to write in it sporadically during the Choctaw removal itself in 1832 and again in 1837. Later, Pitchlynn would become the Principal Chief of the Choctaw Tribe.

A few years after the last entry in Pitchlynn's diary, Charles Dickens happened to meet him on a riverboat in Ohio, and he characterized him at some length in his *American Notes*. Dickens' portrait of Pitchlynn is tinted by the myth of the innocent embattled in a lost paradise, the wise and dignified representative of a doomed, idealized race—an emblem of the Native American that predated *The Last of the Mohicans* and will live on beyond *Dances with Wolves*. Something of the real Pitchlynn peeks through Dickens' mythical haze, but the diary here presented, and the story it tells, affords a more complex portrait.

In this year of memorializing the half-millenium since Columbus arrival, we would be well served by learning more of the true chronicles of Native Americans, rather than casually turning them into symbols of this or that—brutal savages or helpless sufferers, idealized ecologists, or dwellers in Eden cast out by some inevitable force. Out of the gritty stuff of history we can perhaps carve a finer momument.

SM

"Get me some English majors RIGHT AWAY! We've got an unexploded plot device in the World Trade Center!"

THE TELEGRAPH RELAY STATION
/ Norman Lavers

T HREE DAYS BEYOND the fort on the stage, following the
line of telegraph poles like a spider slowly clambering its web.
The dry grass prairie is sere and burned looking, like brown skin
with a worn ghost of hair on it, the buffalo far to the south at
this time of year—Thanksgiven day—but packs of white wolves
standing and looking at us curiously. What can they find to eat?
All morning long we look forward to seeing the telegraph relay
station, mainly because there is utterly nothing else to see. That
is the place where I will depart from my two fellow passengers
and wait for the stage that comes through from the north, and
will take me south to my destination.

There 't is! Curly hollers back down to us, and we bump each
other to be first to crane our heads out the window, squinting
our eyes into the dust and bits of broke-off dry grass. It's a low
cabin of adobe, the same color of the bare dirt, but with a steep
peaked roof to shrug off the winter snows, no trees or bushes
about it.

When we get closer, we see extra poles at the front, where
the telegraph wire we are following goes into the building, then
comes back out on the other side and rejoins the line of poles
continuing straight ahead. But it is a crossroads, and the wire
from the line of poles coming down from the north also enters
the building, then reemerges and continues south, following the
southern road.

Well before we reach it, a man has emerged from the front
door, a fur cap with ear flaps, buttoning his coat as he runs
and stumbles towards us. He reaches us, shouting happily up at
Curly, then walks alongside, directly in our dust, escorting us to
the station. He is looking in the window at us, face gawped in
grin, waving to us repeatedly, so that we must answer his wave
half a dozen times. I see that tears are streaming his joyful face.

We crawl out, patting the trip dust off our coats, out of our
beards, beating our hats against our legs, unkinking our stiff backs,
stamping our frozen feet on the hard ground. He ushers us in
to the welcome of a hot stove, takes our coats from us, thrusts
steaming tin cups of coffee at us, burning our hands and our lips

on the metal, the whole room filled with the savory smell of fresh buffalo steaks cooking. Thanksgiven, he says. He sits us at the rough table, neatly set, and while we eat he stands and watches us, thrilled, like a child looking at his new Christmas presents, though the only gift we have for him is our brief human presence, before we carry on in our different directions.

I bid Curly, and my two fellow passengers—friends now, after two weeks of travel—adieu. And the coach, which seemed to roll so slowly when we were in it, is out of sight and hearing within minutes, and there is no sound but the steady wind whistling in the overhead wires. I turn to my host—I will be staying overnight, my connecting coach arriving the next day noon—and he is not looking down the now empty road. He is frankly staring at me, a smile hovering about his mouth, with something of the expectancy of a new groom regarding his fresh bride. I feel a little stirring of alarm, though I am certain the man is quite harmless.

Will you have more to eat? he asks eagerly.

I couldn't force in another bite, thank you very much.

My pleasure, my pleasure. No need to thank me. More coffee, then?

Yes, that would be lovely, I say (I am already sloshing).

We sit across from each other at the table. With his bulky cap and coat off, my host is a small slight mostly bald man. He watches me for any least chance to serve me, leaps to the stove to set a straw ablaze to light my cigar.

He cannot seem to stop talking.

O it's lonely lonely here, he says, then bursts out laughing.

I can well imagine.

You can't. No no I didn't mean that to sound so short and dismissing. I am sure you are a compassionate, deep imagining man, I can see it in the kindness of your eyes. But you simply can't. Nothing here to see, day in day out. The stages come by once or twice a week while the roads are open, but in winter— O, it's too terrible. Nothing, my friend, nothing. The howling wind. The endless blizzards. There is a strong rope that leads to the outhouse, though it is only fifty paces from here. It looks ridiculous now, but in another month, when the snows come, it will be dire necessity. You cling to it all the way out, and cling to it all the way back. Take your hand off it in a white-out blizzard and at once you lose direction. You can't see even your feet and you lose sense of up and down, so that you topple over. O it's too—ridiculous! Again he bursts out laughing.

I have my mouth open to say, How do you keep your sanity? But thinking better of it, say, Have you no partner here?

Ha, that is a story indeed. I had a partner when I first came here. In fact, he taught me everything. I could no more send or receive a wire than talk to the man in the moon, but he taught me. I came in, just like you, on the stage one day. Well, I had no job, no real prospects, so he convinced me to stay. In our very first winter together, he went out one night for a call of nature, and I never saw hide nor hair again. I suspect he wandered off on purpose, the skunk, just so's not to face it anymore. Anyway, I found out next spring he made it to an Indian village, where he spent the winter. But nothing could ever drag him back here again. Me, I went through the rest of that endless winter—I remember it as almost always nighttime—completely alone. All that kept mind together was the messages coming in for me to transmit onwards, and the answers returning. That world of ticking sounds under my finger became like my family. I became like a blind man with only my sense of touch and hearing to connect me to the outside. But a wonderful sort of blind man who could be in all places at once, hear everybody talking everywhere. The next summer I got me an Indian woman to stay here, not very bright or very good looking, but a sweet enough soul. But in the winter when I needed her most, she up and died on me, and I was alone again. The summers are not so bad, because sometimes, like now, I get a soul to talk to—And say! What a treat you are!—but the winters! O! O! O!—and here is another one spang upon us. Wait! Here's a call coming in.

I hear the loud tickety-tack. He rushes to his desk, takes the stub of pencil off his ear, and begins writing down characters on his notepad. Then he is tappity-tapping on his own big finger key. He waits, more tickety-tack, more writing, then he turns to me, a broad smile on his face.

It was for you, he says. They got a heavy snow up north—early this year—and your coach will be delayed a couple of days till they can dig out. Cross your fingers. If they get more snow and can't get through, there won't be no more runs till next spring.

The bitter smell of coffee awakes me. He is shoving the tin cup into my face. There is a candle lit on the table, and the fire is roaring, though he must have built it up quiet as a mouse to keep from disturbing me. It is still crisp in the room, and the sun is not up so it should be pitch dark out, but instead there is a sort of curious luminescence from the windows, a cold glowing. The wind has stopped and it is utterly still.

You'd better come have a look at this, my host says. He still has that smile playing about his mouth, the bride-groom eagerness. I struggle into my trousers, my bare feet on the frozen floor, and come with him to the window and look out.

Immense soft white flakes are curving down swiftly. They are already four inches deep on the railing outside. The sky is brightening, but there is absolutely nothing to see except sheet after sheet of swirling flakes until all is lost in an amorphous whiteness.

By noon it is a foot of snow with no surcease, by sunset two feet, and the flakes are falling even faster as I make another trip to the outhouse, my boots going clear to the ground through the soft wet snow at every step. I spend the day pacing the four corners of the tiny cabin, trying to stifle my panic. I have already read twenty times till I have memorized the stage schedule, which seems to be the only reading matter in the building. How could I have been so stupid, so improvident? How can I even contemplate six months in this worse-than-a-penitentiary? My host watches me eagerly, rushing to serve me any way he can. That old expression, "keeping body and soul together," has suddenly a problematical cast.

I toss and turn all night thinking: This early freak of storm will melt off in a day or two and I can still escape, but each time I sneak over to the window, it is still pouring out of the heavens. By morning it is four feet deep, and though there was little to see before in the wide empty plain, now there is nothing whatever, a mere blank and formless white clear to the extent of vision. I sit by the fire in stunned despair, refusing breakfast, and then dinner, only drinking coffee, and gnawing at a piece of biskett to save gnawing at my own knuckle.

My host is busy. Calls are coming in constantly for him to relay north or south, east or west, people stranded in the sudden storm, connections missed, meetings aborted, a wedding cancelled.

I am a reading man, I say in agony. Is there nothing whatever in this cabin to read?

His eyes light up, and he goes at once to his cedar chest, rummages frantically, throwing out clothing in all directions, comes up with a large cloth package, unties the strings fastening it, reaches in and comes up with his treasure—and a true treasure it seems when I realize what it is. It is an immense family Bible. A whole great nation's compendium of wisdom and philosophy and morality which, such is the state of my spiritual nature, I had never been able to read past the begats. Here indeed is hope I could spend some of my time profitably. He pulls the table over by the fire, pulls up the most comfortable chair to it, and sets the great heavy tome flat on the table, and brings the lanthorn up by it.

I am in no hurry. I mean to savor every word, mull it over, draw from it its full substance, chew it and digest it. I open to the title page, where it is inscribed with his family name, and with the date of purchase, going back to a time before we were the United States. And there, one after the other, the names of various of his antecedents, all on the male side, and later on, to judge by the dates, brothers of his, and finally his own name some two or three times, and after each signature, the date, and a solemn pledge never again to imbibe in spiritous liquors.

I turn to page one, and read: In the beginning God created the heav'n & the earth. & the earth was without form, & voyde; & darkness was upon the face of the deep. & the Spirit of God moved upon the face of the waters.

It stops snowing for a few days, but it does not melt. Only, the four feet settles into one foot, and develops sufficient crust that it will support our snowshoes and we can tramp about with a gun looking for game, though there is none. Then it snows more feet, then settles, and so on. Each morning one or other of us digs out the back door and the path to the outhouse. There is a covered porch that leads to the barn with our food supplies and fuel (dried buffalo chips). The front door is blocked by drifted snow which comes halfway up the windows, reducing what little light there is from outside.

I am once more bogged down in the begats. My host knows from his experience that it is best for us to pursue our separate occupations, only coming together to talk at meals, and after supper at night when we sit together about the fire. He is surprisingly busy relaying messages during the day. In quiet moments he rolls and smokes cigarettes and sits by the partially occluded window. I scribble notes in my notebooks, try to plow forward in the Bible. We make shift to pass the day, he much better at it than I.

At meals now he is serene and I am the one who cannot stop talking. We have told each other every last wrinkle of our life histories. He seems tranquilly happy at the unexpected boon of my company. For my own part I feel, at moments, a scream starting from somewhere deep in my bowels. I think, if I hear one more tapity tap from his tinny machine I will launch my head through each of his window panes in turn. I envision lifting up the stove and shaking its burning faggots out on the floor. I daydream artillery barrages.

He is sensitive to my moods, watching me from the tail of his eye. I stand up with the idea of taking the shotgun outside and merely firing it off. He rises too, with a smile, and says, Come here, you might as well learn how this operates.

I am told about inventor Samuel F. B. Morse and his ingenious international code based on long and short sounds electrically transmitted down hundreds of miles of wire. At each point where resistance in the wire begins to slow and weaken the signal, there is a relay station where an operator "reads" the message, then sends it off fresh on a new wire to continue its journey. In this way virtually instantaneous communication can connect thousands of square miles of territory, in time our entire nation.

He takes a page of my notebook, and with his pencil writes down the code for me. A ._; B _...; C _._.; and so on. I have a quick memory and study it all day until I have it by heart. Now I listen with new interest in the tickety tack, but it is too fast, I can't catch the rhythm, I can't break in to see where it starts and stops. He laughs at my frustration—I was the same, he says. In a quiet moment he says: Get your pad and take this—and with his pencil he taps a message on the wood of the table, slowly and carefully. He has to repeat it several times before I get it all.

W-H-A-T-H-A-T-H-G-O-D-W-R-O-U-G-H-T

Then I try, and, haltingly, referring back to my notebook, I send the same message back to him, then again, doing it swifter.

The next morning there is a purpose to get up. I sit at the desk beside him, taking down the messages on my own notepad, then comparing with him. At first I only get a letter or a word here and there, but then more and more. Finally I get an entire message perfectly. He jumps to his feet, I jump to my feet, and we embrace.

You've got the calling, he says. Those with the calling catch on at once, the others never.

We send messages back and forth by pencil tapping, and finally he says I am ready to transmit a message. The first is a botch, I am so frightened and tentative on the big electric key, and he has to come in after me and re-send it. But then I get the touch— he's right, I do have a gift—and I am able to send slowly and accurately, then faster, not so fast as him by a long shot, but tolerable.

One day he says, you're my partner now. I'm not afraid to obey a call of nature, or take a snooze, or go out scouting for game, because I know you are here to back me.

To prove it he leaves me for an hour to ramble around on his snow shoes, and messages start coming in at once, and a couple of times I have to ask for repeats, and a couple of times I have to apologize and make a second transmission, and at first I am sweating profusely—but by the time he gets back I feel competent and professional.

Nevertheless, it is a long time before I am relaxed enough to begin paying attention to the messages themselves. At first they are mere alphabetical counters I am receiving and relaying on, and that takes every ounce of my concentration. But little by little they begin to flesh out into words, become voices that I hear in my head almost as I hear spoken voices. The speakers begin to take on human form in my mind. And—since we have no sense of the passage of time here, and our minds seem to sleep between transmissions—even though answers come a day or several days after an original message, in our senses, suspended in our memories, the replies seem to come close after, as if we were overhearing actual conversations.

TO ED WOBURN AT FT CLAPTON HAPPY BIRTHDAY THIS DAY YOUR FOND BROS TOM MOSE JOSIAH WALTER

TO ANYONE INDIAN TERRITORY WORD OF MY HUSBAND JIM THOMPSON REWARD ELIZ THOMPSON

TO ANYONE FT CLAPTON AREA OR SOUTH WIDOW 38 HARD WORKER SAVINGS LOOK ALRIGHT PLUMP SEEK MAN W LAND PURP MATRIMONY FLO BUSKIRK

TO RICK CRUM AT PAWNY CORNERS CANT GET THRO
SNOW SEE YOU NEXT YR BIG DRINKING PARTY THEN SAM

TO FLO BUSKIRK AT FT LEAVENWORTH AM 33 HAVE 138
ACR SOME CATTLE HORSES PROSPECTS GOOD SLIGHT LIMP
FT CLAPTON AREA ED WOBURN

TO FLO BUSKIRK AT FT LEAVENWORTH HAVE 5000 ACR
MANY CATTLE HORSES TANNERY MILL GOOD WATER FT
CLAPTON AREA AM 73 CY MCCLINTOCK

TO FLO BUSKIRK AT FT LEAVENWORTH AM 21 GOOD
LOOKING PAWNY CORNERS AREA BUY LAND W YR SAVINGS
RICK CRUM

Wait, my host says. Don't send those last three on.

What do you mean?

We've got to think about them first. If you sent her the one of
that probably worthless flighty pup Rick Crum, think what will
happen. She's newly widowed. I know what that's like when your
mate is suddenly gone. You're no longer getting what your body
is used to, your blood is up in you. She might make a terrible
even if fully understandable mistake.

I start laughing. So—what?—do we only send on the one from
the well-heeled Cy McClintock?

No. That's no good either. After her loss, she may be down,
she may have lost confidence in the future, she might make a
cautious choice for the old geezer, and get trapped into a marriage
with no tenderness in it. She's still relatively young. It's got to be
Ed Woburn. He's a good man. See how much his brothers like
him. Just send that one on.

You can't be serious! We don't know any of this. "Slight limp"
may mean wooden leg. We can't take this kind of responsibility
for someone else's life. We just have to send the offers on and let
her make her own choice. People have to be free to make their
own mistakes. That's what life's about.

You don't know this place as well as I do. That's not how we
work things here. This is my relay station.

TO JAY CHALMERS AT COTTONWOOD GROVE DADDY SO
GLAD TO HEAR YOU ARE ALIVE AND WELL WHEN CAN
YOU RETURN ALWAYS LOVE YR DTR CLEMENTINE

Don't send that one either.

Why, for goodness' sake?

I'll answer it from here, he says. And while I watch stupefied he taps out:

TO CLEMENTINE CHALMERS IN ST. LOUIS CANT COME THIS YR MY DEAR CAUGHT BY EARLY SNOW NEXT SPRING FOR SURE FONDLY DADDY.

He looks at me sheepishly. She's been sending inquiries for her dad for a year. He's dead out there somewhere, or abandoned her. I couldn't stand her waiting so piteously for him, so I—well I manufactured some answers from him.

What're you going to do if he really answers sometime?

That already happened on another case, a woman looking for her husband. What a nightmare.

Do you mean you do this all the time?

Do you think I've probably made a mistake? he asks.

I sure do, I say, then wish I hadn't answered so quick when I see his face wince with pain and fear, and then slowly sort of cave in.

I didn't intend it to be that way. (To my astonishment he is blubbering, in tears). I just wanted to help, to be encouraging, to do something to ward off the god-awful loneliness and isolation. Now I've got dozens of them, whole families I've invented and put into contact, marriages that are going forward or being restored when one or other probably don't exist. I'm in so deep I can't get out of it anymore, I have to keep inventing more and more people in a big web and somehow keep them all separated from each other, and separated in my own mind. Once I caught myself making up a reply to another person I had made up. O me, what have I done.

He drops his head into his hands and looks so desolated I reach around and pat his shoulder.

Then he throws his head back up.

You were absolutely right, he says, I should have left them free in the first place. What do you figure I should do now?

Well, for a start, don't do any new ones. And for the others— and the whole great complex mess of it suddenly comes present to me, and I cannot stop a groan, which my host, who has been hanging eagerly to my words, matches, and sinks his head back down on the table again—For the others, I go on, I guess you can't say anything now, but you'll just have to start disengaging 'em. Kill off this one, marry off that one.

O that's so easy to say, he moans, but how can I really do it? These are human beings I have got myself involved with, how can I let them down so brutally?

You've just got to, I say. We'll work on it together. I'll stand by you, and we'll think up something case by case.

I've got a call of nature, he says, and heads for the door.

Your coat and hat, I say. (The blizzard has been blowing nonstop for two days.)

O. Yes, he says, and puts them on.

He pulls the door open, snow swirling in and scattering across the floor, then closes it carefully behind him.

As soon as he is gone, calls start coming in.

TO FLO BUSKIRK AT FT LEAVENWORTH AM 41 WIDOWER HAVE LAND W WATER CATTLE SOME WHEAT AT CEDAR SPRS NR CLAPTON AREA HARD WORK BUT GOOD LIFE WE HAVE BOTH BEEN HURT BUT WE CAN START AGAIN PLEASE COME JIM THOMPSON

That one sounds so good I am sure my host would have no objection to it, so I relay it forward. I had not yet sent the other three proposals, and I catch myself thinking there will be no harm waiting a bit longer, till she has had a chance to respond to this good one. But I realize I am falling into the same trap my host fell into, and so I send those three as well, giving her all four to make up her own mind about. But I admit to myself I am pulling for Jim Thompson.

More calls come in.

TO ANYONE INDIAN TERRITORY WORD OF MY HUSBAND JIM THOMPSON REWARD ELIZ THOMPSON

I have relayed it forward before the import strikes me like a blow to the head. That son of a bitch conniving bigamist Jim Thompson! Where is my host now? We've got to discuss this one.

But he does not come in. It's been an hour.

He wouldn't! That's not funny.

I put on my coat and hood and wrap my muffler about my face, leaving only the tiniest slit for my eyes. I pull open the door. New snow has already drifted in deep. The pathway is already nearly filled in, with almost no trace of his footsteps. The wind is blowing hard pellets of snow-ice directly into me, striking me like gravel. I get the door closed and plough my way forward, clinging to the lifeline with one mitten. Close to my eyes I can see the flurrying movement of the driving pellets, but farther than a foot from my eyes I can see nothing. It is midday, but it might as well be midnight, except that instead of pitch dark it is snow white. I lose my vertical equilibrium and fall to the side, for a terrifying instant almost losing contact with the line, but my fingers get a death grip on it, and I pull myself back up, though up has little meaning for me. I flounder on. I am gasping, and every time my breath rushes out, it builds a little deeper mask of ice on the wool material of my muffler right before my nose and lips and in my rising panic, that I seek to push back down, I wonder if I am slowly walling myself into a cage of my own frozen breath. I feel I have gone a mile forward, though I know the line is scarce thirty yards. I want very much to turn back, but that will answer nothing, so I continue doggedly forward, until my head strikes with a bump against the door of the outhouse. I have to dig with my hands now to clear a little space to drag the door open. I feel about inside even putting my hand the length of my arm down the hole itself. Empty. Empty. The scream is inside me like a bubble moving about in my body for an opening out of which to discharge itself.

My own path has already filled in, but it is easier returning to the cabin with the wind behind me. I have to brush away the snow that has blown inside the door before I have room to shut it fast. I hear the tickety tacking as I pull off my stiff coat and throw it to the floor. I am already taking it down in my head before I get to my pad of paper and begin writing it.

TO JIM THOMPSON AT CEDAR SPRS HAVE 1000 FROM LIFE INS YES I HAVE BEEN HURT BUT I HEAR KINDNESS IN YR VOICE HOPING FLO BUSKIRK

Grimly, I relay the message on, but every instinct tells me I should not have.

The answer when it comes is so cynical I cannot force my fingers onto the key, cannot enter into complicity with him in that way, so at least for the time being I set the message aside:

TO FLO BUSKIRK AT FT LEAVENWORTH 1ST BREAK IN

SNOW I COME TO FT LEAVENWORTH IF I SUIT WE CAN
MARRY TRANSFER FUNDS ETC I HEAR YR BEAUTIFUL SOUL
YR JIM

I hear a scratching at the wall, my heart leaps and I race to the
door, but it is not my host returned, it is a rat trying to scratch his
way in. The walls and ceiling are filled with them. We hear them
all night trying to get in when we are trying to sleep. And when
the wind stops for a moment, the wolves commence howling in
the most hideous manner. We see nothing outside anymore, the
snow drifted above the tops of the windows.

I come back and look at Jim Thompson's diabolically clever
hypocritical messages to that trusting woman, I brood over his
treatment of both those trusting women, his deserted wife still
seeking him, fearing he is in trouble. Anger flares up in me, and
I take action.

TO ELIZ THOMPSON IN ST LOUIS REGRET INFORM HUS-
BAND JIM THOMPSON DIED HERO SAVING CHILDREN FROM
INDIANS LAST WORDS I LOVE YOU ELIZ PLEASE START NEW
LIFE A FRIEND JOHN RINDO

TO FLO BUSKIRK AT FT LEAVENWORTH YOU FAT COW 1000
NOT ENOUGH WIRE WHEN YOU HAVE 10000 JIM THOMPSON

I am thinking, How could my host be so selfish? I need him
here. I need to talk to him.

TO JOHN RINDO AT PLAINS CROSSING YOU SOUND NICE
CAN I COME TO YOU IN SPRING FOR ADVICE RE STARTING
NEW LIFE YR NEW FRIEND ELIZ THOMPSON

Hm, that was a short period of mourning. Perhaps there was
more equality in that marriage than I suspected.

Then a message comes down from the far north, with a notation
that it has already been forwarded down from farther north from
the Athabasca

TO ELIZ THOMPSON DEAREST AM ALIVE AND WELL CDNT
WRITE WHILE A FAILURE BUT NOW IVE HIT IT LEAD AND
SILVER WE ARE ON EASY STREET DID IT ALL FOR YOU
COMING BACK TO MY DARLING IN THE SPRING ALWAYS

FAITHFUL LOVE JIM

I pace round and round the four corners of the single room. It is abundantly clear that Jim Thompson cannot send messages to widow Buskirk from nearby Cedar Springs, and at the same time send messages to his wife Elizabeth from up in the high Athabasca, and be one and the same person. He could, however, send both these messages if he was in fact two unrelated, and perhaps quite decent and honorable people who happen to share, by coincidence, the same name.

This comes next:

TO FLO BUSKIRK AT FT LEAVENWORTH WHY HAVENT YOU REPLIED ALL I HAVE I WANT TO SHARE W YOU EAGERLY JIM

Now how do I send that one on? Especially when this comes:

TO CY MCCLINTOCK AT FT CLAPTON AM SERIOUSLY CONSIDERING YR PROPOSAL PLEASE SEND MORE DETAILS LAND AND HOLDINGS RESPECTFULLY FLO BUSKIRK

I try this:

TO ELIZ THOMPSON REGRET TERRIBLE MISTAKE BUT HAPPY OUTCOME YR HUSBAND ALIVE AND WELL DIFFERENT JIM THOMPSON KILLED YOU WILL HEAR FROM TRUE HUSBAND SHORTLY WITH GOOD NEWS SINCERELY JOHN RINDO

The rats scratch at the walls, the ceiling, under the floor, trying to get in. The tickety tacking starts up again.

TO JOHN RINDO AT PLAINS CROSSING YOU STILL SOUND NICE HUSBAND ALWAYS A FAILURE CRAMPS MY STYLE MUST SEE YOU SOONEST DEAR BOY THINKING OF MY NEW LIFE FONDLY ELIZ THOMPSON

I do not feel very happy about it, but it is time to send forward his news of lead and silver and easy street. I do so. The next message is not long in coming, and not unexpected.

TO JOHN RINDO AT PLAINS CROSSING FORGET ALL

FORMER CORRESPONDENCE MY WONDERFUL HUSBAND
RETURNING I AM SO HAPPY RESPECTFULLY ELIZ THOMPSON

Is what I create worse than what I leave alone? Should I never
have started? Should I refuse to go on? Around about is the white
whirling chaos of the void, the bitter cold of non-being. Is that
better, as my host evidently came to believe? My host frozen into
whiteness himself, unless he made it to the Indians. The small
gnawing animals scurry in the walls and chew chew chew to
breach the thin envelope into my warm room.

The tickety tack is going again.

TO JAY CHALMERS AT COTTONWOOD GROVE DADDY LIFE
IS SO HARD PLEASE MY FATHER SPEAK TO ME ELSE HOW
CAN I KNOW YOU EXIST ALWAYS LOVE YR DTR CLEMENTINE

Norman Lavers holds 1991 creative writing fellowships from the Arkansas Arts
Council and the National Endowment for the Arts.

GOREPAC / *Will Baker*

I'VE HAD A LONG day with the sharks, and Audrey is exhausted after a basement workout. It's Time for Two time. Bliss out with a drink, take stock, relate. So we make the arrangements: Gabe shooed off to the neighbors, answering machine on duty, and Falafel has his kitty kibbles.

Aud puts together a tray: chips, salsa, a Miller and a Blue Mountain Spring Water, one frosty mug. My thing, to keep glass in the freezer for that extra edge.

"I'm benching eight nineties," Aud says as she folds down to the rug, parking the tray between us. She makes a sound like a punctured tire.

"Fantastic. You look great." I lay a ribbon of gold along the side of the glass, tilted just enough to give me a creamy head. "Downright *bad*."

She is pleased. But I am not lying. Aud looks tight and springy as a coed, though forty is now in sight. She's sweaty at the moment, still a bit stoked. Sometimes that turns me on. Damp curls and a flush and so on. Only when she wears a summer dress, and leans over to lever up a bit of dip with a celery section, you see too much delt.

"Flattery will get you absolutely everything you want. You cad." She winks just as she chugs the Blue Mountain, an odd effect. I watch her throat working, wait for her to uncouple, give her unladylike burp and a-a-a-h. Aud has gusto.

"*Everything*?"

"Sure. Within the bounds of middle class pornography. You know. No chickens or sheep."

We laugh at this line from an old joke. For a while we dab and shovel salsa, taking care not to break a chip, which in our house means gofering the next round of drinks. Except for the forced air and a power mower somewhere down the block, it's very quiet.

"So?" Audrey finally says. She is not looking at me. She is picking at the Blue Mountain label with her long thumbnail.

"So. So I called him." I drink from the mug, feel the ice crystals on my lower lip. I wish she had waited a little. It's not often this calm, just us two.

I take a deep breath. This is an effort. "He says come in twice a week. All of us."

"Sweet Jesus." Aud's eyes are closed, her face absolutely empty and no longer flushed. "I *just* took on the Arts Council thing. What does he say?"

"I was talking on the modular, in traffic. We didn't get into it. A suggestion. Just a suggestion." I drink swiftly, deeply.

"Did you tell him? The whole story?"

"Aud, I was on my way to work. Twenty-five minutes, full-bore freeway, two other calls to make."

She turns her head ninety degrees and addresses the corner of the living room. "Which, I wonder, did he make first?"

I open my mouth, then close it in the next heartbeat. Push pause. I have learned.

She turns back to me, and then in a moment she is shaking her head slowly, fingers on her temples. "Baby, baby. I'm sorry. Not fair." She lifts one hand away, holds it out to me. "Touch."

I take her cool fingers and press them to my forehead, my cheek; then let her draw my hand in and do the same. We both close our eyes and image our best moment together, a technique we learned at a retreat before Gabe was born. For me the beach at Cabo under a full moon, us naked and sandy and salty, a thermos of margaritas.

"Listen, I would do *anything*, absolutely. He's our kid, our own flesh and blood, what can I say?" I am squeezing her hand and she winces, only half-comically. "I mean, we *are* aware of the problem."

We release and she wiggles her fingers, making a quick claw. "For a fat guy, you still have a grip."

I smile, but the sense of effort is still there. Nor am I, actually, what you would call a fat guy. A basic athletic frame, but my work doesn't exactly fight spread. I produce ads for the biggest furniture chain in the country. Exciting work and a very good salary, but believe me it exacts a physical toll.

"The masturbation is normal," Aud says, snaring and bending one index finger with her other hand.

"Except for his age. Age and development."

"He's developing. Come *on*, baby."

The tone is aggressive maternal. I don't answer because she knows as well as I do that Gabe is way small, uncoordinated, and wears thick dweeb spectacles. Almost fourteen and no sign of the growth spurt or new hair, his voice still locked in treble.

He'll throw a ball if I lay a big trip on him, or leave his computer and go outside if someone threatens to unplug it. The same way a dog slinks when you roll up the newspaper.

Aud forks a second finger into her fist. "A rich fantasy life. That's not bad."

I still don't answer. She sees what I think in my wry half smile.

"Although, I mean, I grant he does too much video. You were right about that. But..." She lets air out of another tire.

"Sneaking into our room and going through stuff, this is not a rich fantasy life." I hold up three fingers. "Or tattooing yourself with a pin."

I am a blunt person. At a certain point I come out with it. It is my nature, part of my belief that life has no margins, gives nobody extra space. All you've got is what you create, and that's why I care about the little extras: the mugs in the freezer, sheepskin seatcovers, fresh cilantro.

"We can't be absolutely sure."

"I'm sure."

Sure enough that I have the Magnum rehidden in a locked drawer and all our personal tapes likewise in the garage tool cabinet. I am also a decisive person. So is Aud, actually, everywhere except with Gabe. That's *her* rich fantasy life.

"I don't think they're connected. I mean, he's curious, maybe. Wants confirmation or something. To know what we actually *do*. Snitching from the tapes would be hot stuff for a kid. His dinky little masochism is something else." She cocks her head, purses her lips, reconsidering. "I mean sex and violence are always connected *somehow*, I guess. We learned that much."

She is thinking about our first sessions with our first therapist, all the talk about Deep Screen syndrome, libido hallucination and so on. The theory was Gabe projected his conflicts into the games, and so blew them away. Under the zooming and darting bloboids was a shadow play of prepubescent feelings.

I've never told her precisely how I got on to the whole thing, about coming into his room in my stocking feet so he didn't hear me. Seeing him with his hand in his pocket, hunched over, the screen blossoming with fire and cracked by lightning. He was making a sound like a puppy trapped under a rug.

To this day I don't know why I reacted as I did. I reversed like one of those film strips run backwards. In the hall I took a long breath and then came on again, setting my heels down solidly. He was sitting up this time, pale and damp and cool, and it was hi pop, matter-of-fact, just killing time, zapping a few alien freaks. After that I started to really observe. That's when I began to think, you have a really weird kid, buddy, and not in the casual sense.

"Channel change." Aud puts herself in a half lotus, back very straight. This is another technique from one of the retreats. I close my eyes and clear my mind.

After three slow breaths she says, "How's the Spacemaster doing?"

"Picking up. Kensington Mall branch sold six on Wednesday." I finish my beer, which has gotten too warm now anyway. "Twelve hundred a pop."

"O-o-h! Daddy! Love it. Maybe *we* should get one." She hunches her shoulders and wrinkles up her nose, the crazy little girl. "Can you ball in it?"

I look away. Aud can channel change almost too fast. The retreat leader said one in a thousand. But sometimes it's like blinding, and I don't know which way to move.

Falafel pads into the room, licking his needle teeth, fourteen pounds of sensual eunuch in splendid winter coat. He positions himself between us, stretching seductively, but Aud pushes him away and he slouches to the sofa.

"Maybe Christmas," I say. Most of a year away. By then the hormones could hit; Gabe could snap out of it and save us money. I mostly think that's the answer. They're all little geeks until they get some balls and bone, discover the Big Rush.

But if we go to doctor Minh twice a week I'll have to hustle more Spacemaster spots. It's a great recliner, top of the line, but still a bit overpriced. A complete leisure unit: six-way tilt, built-in remotes and swing trays, hot and cold cup wells, timer, the works. A total security fantasy, actually modeled on the Shuttle Station command module seat. We should pump that angle again in the new ads.

"Come on, break a chip, somebody." I twirl my empty mug on one finger.

"Get some exercise, you snail." Aud rolls her empty over the pile carpet to me. "Screwdriver me this time."

I am up and three steps toward the kitchen when she adds, "Then I want to show you something."

When I get back with her driver and my new frosty mug the TV is on and Aud is out of the room. AAW is playing, I presume because Gabe left it there. I set down the drinks and pick up the remote, thinking maybe I'll go to Sportsorama or catch the quotes on CashFlash. But there is an update running on Tundra Terror, some action south of Baikal, apparently, since Friday. I am just wondering where Aud is when she comes back, a portable deck and keyboard in her arms.

"Leave it." She signals with her eyes at the remote in my hand. "And patch this in for me."

I hoist eyebrows, but she doesn't say anything, just shoves the gear into my chest. It's two minutes to connect the keyboard to deck to monitor, during which I half-listen to a talking head, which is giving the stats for a new phosphor tracer called the Serpent of Light. It can go around corners apparently, a white fire that splits and weaves, hunting flesh.

I sit down again, move the tray aside to make room for the keyboard. I notice how dirty the keys are, a clue to how much Gabe pounds them. Power on, the image on the screen flakes and wobbles for an instant. The talking head has been replaced by a bare landscape flowing, racing like a river beneath a G-20 Striker which is really hugging the terrain, mowing dandelions. Superpower hard rock gives the flow a rhythm.

"So?" I raise my mug, glance at Aud. She is back in the half lotus and now lifts the keyboard and sets it in her lap.

"Wait. Just a second. I'm not sure I can get this the way I've seen him do it, but...." She is watching the screen intently, wiggling her fingers in anticipation.

"I know he watches this shit too much. But so do most boys. It's a phase."

We've already discussed this, more than once. I'm disappointed that Aud tries to make her point this melodramatic way. They've done the research. They say it actually demystifies aggression for kids, and everybody knows that it's good training for those who actually get into a PeaceKeeper career. But Gabe as a skyjockey is, frankly, a completely impossible idea.

In the river of earth peeling away under the Striker a cluster of dark flecks appears. They're past in a blink, before the whole horizon rolls, slides away. We boost straight up for a couple of seconds and then the world rolls back and the screen is a map under a grid, accelerating toward us. I see the flecks again, inside the grid which gyrates and steadies.

Boring, so far. I glance at Aud again. She's still concentrating, pinching her upper lip between her teeth, fingers poised. We've watched this same kill a thousand times. Maybe even this exact one. They splice in old stuff all the time, matching the beat.

I watch once in a while, and everyone does if there is some real major now action. Jungle Sweep, for example, was good for almost a year. Otherwise it's all testing systems, maneuvers, the talking heads, and reruns. Every so often a docuhistory, which I actually prefer. They go back even before the first Desert Storm show, to Vietnam and the World Wars, which are a kick because of the clunky old machines.

Serpent of Light is launched. It looks like any number of others going in, a small, nosey meteor. The black flecks have gathered at the center of the screen. When the meteor touches them there is the usual sudden, splashy radiance. On the soundtrack a tremendous cliff of a chord.

"Yeah, okay. Here!" Aud arrests the bloom of light, folds it back into a point. We are out of real time. When she runs it again she does a slo-mo enhancement and magnification. In timed jerks the terrain under the grid leaps closer to us.

The music has become a deep grinding vibration, somewhere between the biggest pipe of an organ and an earthquake. Even with enhancement the image is degenerating, the flecks turn into patches of shimmering dots and the incoming missile is a giant white mold consuming a whole corner of the screen.

"Aud," I say, trying for gentle patience. "Sharing is important no question, but—"

"Wait. Watch, baby. *Watch* this."

She adds color separation, picks up the contrast. The kind of thing done now in kindergarten for art hour. I feel a funny, sudden tightness in my throat. But I do watch, and all at once in the play of form and primary color I see, between the two tanks, a patch of darkness with legs, four legs. And next to it another stick figure, reminding me again of kindergarten, a smear with a knob at one end and two feet....

"Okay, okay!" Aud is excited. I hear it in her voice, the keys clicking over the low thunder on the soundtrack, but this time I don't look at her. The shadows are expanding and disintegrating at the same time, yet somehow for a microsecond their outline is clear to me, the way the outline of an oncoming truck materializes out of fog. Two tanks, two people, and a herd of goats.

But in the next microsecond the mold begins to spread and unravel. Incandescent worms crawl swiftly over and into the forms on the screen, swelling and discoloring them. Something like the heaving boils and geysers of thermonuclear magma on the surface of the sun. Or those animated electron micro sequences of a virus eating a cell's brains out.

Aud gives a little whimper of awe. She is running a bite back and forth, the instant when the glowing white worms devour the tanks and goats and people. My throat feels definitely hot and thick now. The shapes erupt and erupt and erupt; and then, in a slice of time so thin it exists only as a ghost, I see a face. The mouth stretches, the eyes are already holes, the hair is a swarm of fire. How I cannot say, but I see the face is foreign, Asian, a hun, a girl.

I hear a sound that absolutely scares the living shit out of me. A squeal like a warthog going under a steamroller. I don't even know how I get off the floor and around into a crouch, the beer mug cocked.

It is Falafel. He has screwed himself backwards into the cushions and looks electrocuted, his hair on end, his eyes portholes into hell. He is not looking at the screen, but at me, and when I turn he blows off the couch, across the room and out the door like a furry cannonball.

My spine is a heater coil, glowing and tingling in the base. I hear Aud laugh, then take a long, shuddering breath. Hesitantly she strikes the keys to cut and store, so when I turn back we have lapsed into real time. The America At War theme fades out as a guy in a helmet gives a thumbs up, just before he closes the hatch on a new M-90 Weasel. Click to a whole panel of talking heads in suits.

"Amazing." Aud is trying to smile, looking not quite at me. "I've never seen *either* of you move that fast."

Carefully I sit beside her again, noticing—a wonder—that I have not spilled any beer. The constriction in my throat has eased, but I am trembling and all my inner radar tells me to go slow and be careful. Figure out how I feel, but in stages. I have hooked something big, from the Dreadful, Delightful Deep.

And I know how close this marriage is at this moment, when Aud answers my question just before I am steady enough to ask it.

"We can play it back," she says, "but it won't be there this time."

I do three slow breaths myself. "But you saw it too."

"Yeah. Oh yeah."

Our eyes meet for a moment, then deflect, as if we were two strangers running into each other around a corner. Why, I am asking myself, is this a major matter? Hallucinations happen. Drive too far on too much coffee you get Bigfoot in your headlights. Or low blood sugar, like the fasting seers of old. But my core self, the blunt one with no margins, won't buy it.

"A face. An oriental of some type," I say. "A girl."

Aud bites her lips, nods once.

"That much imaging, over-processing, maybe it's just probability. Autosuggestion." I sound weak even to myself. None of this explains my spine turning into a redhot coil.

"Gabe," she says simply. "I watched him doing it."

I guess what she means and imagine the scene clearly. My kid hunching rapt over the keyboard, Aud spying through a door ajar. Gabe finally aware of her, freezing maybe and then realizing she no longer cares, is hooked too, so he goes on. The two of them at and into the screen. Getting off in sync, maybe. My mind stops.

A commercial is running now. The new Suzuki Commando with double roll bar flips twice down a slope into an alpine cirque. Close shot of the couple inside, her hair in his face, whooping their excitement. They root back up the slope, spraying gravel, toward a magnificent snowy spire. I get a flash of nostalgia for a camping trip some years ago. A sudden, tremendous yearning to drive, stand on a high place, feel a fresh wind in my face.

Crazy, now, because tears come and I have no idea in Christ's world from where. Aud sees them and she's crying too, on my channel instantly and completely. We tip into each other, our foreheads and knees together, so we make a kind of pyramid. This is strange stuff from way deep, and a lot of it. Too much, too much.

I don't know how long we spend in this sea of emotion, maybe only a few seconds, but time and my mind have gone completely elastic. What happens next has the quality of Aud's keyboarding, a fork in reality, because the action goes fast, too fast to control, and yet I am registering everything perfectly, every detail is magnified and every motion is retarded and articulated.

Through my tears and a screen of Aud's hair I see a figure standing behind us. I am moving, rearing, getting a leg under myself. It is almost a replay of the Falafel scare. But I see it is Gabe and I have the fantastic ability to think many, many things at once. I know he has been standing there a while, has been in the house for some time. His look has walked from his keyboard to his mother to me, behind the blank discs of his spectacles.

I know that the soundtrack and our concentration have made us deaf, that we would not have heard the clink of a key or a splintering of wood. I am on my hind legs like a bear and lurching toward him, yet I speak in a soft bluster.

"Gabe," I say, "put that down Gabe."

It is a gun, of course, and he is lifting it, a line, a block, a cone of blackness. I cannot tell if the movement is supplication or defense. I hear the syllables coming from Aud, but they are only a sound like glass breaking. My hand is closing on the barrel and my mouth is open to speak again.

There is something wrong, and I see it first in the small face. His fear winks out, replaced by a smile I have never met before. At the same time I feel it. The rigid little barrel is plastic. A neighbor's toy, an imitation.

But Gabe has read everything in my face, and the smile broadens. It is a smile from long long ago—from the slime, you could say. My son the dweeb now shows teeth, the expression of a thing that has dragged another thing into its hole to feed on.

I experience a flash like a bare bulb being turned on. The plastic gun spins end over end. Gabe is on the floor. I hear his glasses clatter down somewhere. I have hit him. I watch one of his knees cock, then straighten. The sea is inside me now, and it is lava.

Here one branch of time stops altogether. Aud's crying and babbling has ceased as suddenly as the slamming of a door. The house is absolutely still and nobody moves. There is a shuttle of light on the rug, for the set is still on and a metal-bright voice is giving the weather report for the Forces south of Baikal.

This time I feel powerful sympathy for the brave boys and girls over there. I hear their weather for myself, and my family, and this home and how everything will be. Harsh but stimulating. Blazing days and nights bitter, bitter, cold. One moment more I am stunned, the next moment I fastforward. I am roaring, I am singing! I mean I really, really rip it.

Will Baker is the author of several books, including *Track of the Giant*. A collection of stories is due out in 1992 from the University of Missouri Press.

NEW DAYS / *Liz Rosenberg*

Sunlight, strong as
tobacco, that shines
so hard it seems

to push the door
ajar just as
you and I

leaned into a kiss, reached
under clothes to find our
skins. Bright earth,

forgive this
darkness
working in me.

THIS PEACEFUL STREET / *Liz Rosenberg*

On this peaceful street
with its busy cars and twilit headlamps,
no sign of blood, not even road-kill.
Out on the highway, the deer lie sideways.
In markets, the meat sits bloodless in plastic.
Our violence is habitual:
one man might say, Fight to kill
while in hospital basements, the x-rayed
fight only to live.
Across an ocean, young men pace
on either side, scan the night sky
for missiles or angels.

CLOUDS / *Liz Rosenberg*

They hung in the sky, the size of houses,
wilder than the trees.
We lived on our backs, stared up forever past
the shadowy twin towers of our knees
to watch the shapes go by
like carriages without wheels.
And sometimes a chink of gold
would slowly widen
like a door opening—a door! where God
and all his angels strolled.
We'd be about to see them
when our mother's calls would rise
and one by one, so would we,
called home to supper, home to bed
where we would sleep, clouds boiling above our heads.

THE METHOD / *Liz Rosenberg*

What was Maria Montessori thinking
when she crossed the tenement courtyard that first
    morning—
that she could free the children from their chairs,
would free the chairs themselves from the floor?
That morning, she demonstrated
how to blow one's nose, so quietly
the children burst into instant applause.
She wrote, "The child is like the beggar, who looks
    for something
and fails to attain it, who is robbed of his home
and civil rights." The press called her crazy,
outlandish; of course, ugly.
On the next bridge over, the young Mussolini
loped like a starved wolf from locked door
to locked door. Fascist and anti-fascist
sharing the mirror of the Tiber River.
"The chairs might be moved and cleaned every day,
easily lifted even by a child."
One girl, among fruit trees for the first time
cried out in amazement,
"Up there, is a garden of things to eat!"

TERROR / *Liz Rosenberg*

When the first blue fireworks explode
like giant thistles, glassy on the sky
my son is playing a few yards off.
He freezes when it happens, his whole torso shakes
the way I've seen small animals
burst into motion from a dead stand-still
as he runs crying, arms out for his father
like those childish figures in the A.P. photos
real under real skies
who are really dying.

THE SMALLEST GESTURE / *Liz Rosenberg*

Millie's daughter is a thin sixteen,
sick and tired
of waiting for Death to carry her off.
Her medicines shine like jewels
in the wide kitchen window where she sits
patiently, sketching the snow.
And Millie's so busy
chattering, vacuuming—rushing around.
By four she's exhausted, done in for the day.
Fallen into her flowered armchair
in the front parlor dim and square as a box,
Millie's small hand dangles down—
thinking of her daughter
and pointing toward the earth.

INTENSIVE CARE UNIT / *Liz Rosenberg*

Somewhere a TV set is always on,
suspended like a gun three feet above our heads.
A doctor is summoned on the intercom
in a voice calm as a bell,
while a young man screams, thumping the wall—
an overdose—next door; then quiets,
calling hoarsely for his mother.
Down the hall, a child's machines are shut down at last
and an hour later her parents shuffle past our door,
listing like wrecked boats, crying dully,
with a wracked sound, like a cough.
And here is our baby son inside a metal crib.
One pinpoint in the center
of his chest pumps wildly in and out, a moth's wing
whipping the light, frantic for air
and here's the only movie in his room, the bright green
screen of flashing numbers
we stay up all night to watch.

The Catholic priest's our faithful visitor.
He comes to pray, and calls our baby "Buddy,"
which he pronounces "Body,"—oh poor Body,
—like a whippoorwill. The nurses creep along the halls
on soles of crepe; they bring us cups of tea
then come again
to suction our Body's lungs, and he is drowning,
flailing small wrists tied to the rails,
as my great-aunt waved goodbye her last hours on the
    death-cart,
going under. But we invent a game. We tell our son,
who loves to shoot, whom we forbid all guns,
that he can mow this virus down, and his hand
moves feebly in the crib. We play all night—
the flashing green numbers slow like the right spin
on a slot machine, and two days later he is up
in bed, he's wanting juice and cookies, milk, banana,
the nurses smile as we wheel him away

in the going-home stroller,
with a mylar balloon attached. Outside the automatic doors
blue sky, the sun again! Then I remember the old man
whose wife was dying in the next room, behind the bright curtain,
how his face swam toward me like a soul
among the damned, and how our eyes met when he told me
in his trembling baritone, "This place is hell"—
so that we both knew where we were an instant—
and then we touched hands, and it wasn't.

THE NEW LIFE / *Liz Rosenberg*

The big sports announcer afraid to fly and I
sat thigh to thigh watching a cowboy movie
as our train sped through another border town.
He opened the rattling window and leaned out like a
    child
while Old Dodge City shuttered by
half-lit, with yellow dust-brick buildings fluttering in a
    dream.

I sat awake for hours in my sleep
compartment narrow as a phone booth
holding my book before my breast,
watching the Western sky stretch out & fall asleep.
At breakfast, strangers streamed by my famous friend
for autographs & photo tokens; each time he would grin
then bounce his head like a balloon; even hold up
his two, enormous, gaudy superbowl rings as if they
    were
his sons. Then for a long blank time he'd turn away,
his face gone still and stern, as if he'd been erased...

Two black girls in the club car rose
and asked him for a photograph. He was too big, looming
above the frame, and they were short and black.
They had a hungry look, the eyes of dreamers.
I fretted through the camera like a spy,
the two girls by now smiling desperately.
At last I called, "But I can't see you! You're too dark!"
and one girl, exasperated, calm,
said, "Girl, we *is* dark. Take the picture."

My friend dreamed he was dying
in a green light, falling;
but with such sureness of eternity he
woke weightless and peaceful in a wide Ohio field,
fast sailing feet-first through the green mist
toward the East, a backward dancer

---

over the bones of the dead track-makers,
and jarred my hand on the seat beside:
"Why don't we talk about happy things?"

The happy poor were leaning in the wind,
their children sped behind us, waving
to us as delicate, and shallow-rooted
as white blossoms blowing on a high pea fence.

We can make our lives new.

Liz Rosenberg's first book of poems, *The Fire Music*, won the Agnes Starrett Prize.

SHARED VOICES/ *Mary Lee Settle*

PERHAPS THE MOST private experiences are the most universal. I wonder about this. I know that for talented, dreaming children growing up in the South, there is a common shadow line of isolation that is crossed, and that we cannot know for years how strongly it has affected us.

It is that moment when, after seeking, we find someone to share a private language, a private hope, not taste, but true pitch, not an accepted "artistic" experience, but a friend who, in a desert, speaks the language we thought was alien and private. It has happened to every Southern writer whose life I know something about, from Willa Cather, whose first ten years were spent in Virginia, and who wrote over and over, as if she could not shake the experience, about the isolation of growing up and finding that language, that understanding. Flannery O'Connor saw it as an irony, William Faulkner sought it in the past and found it in Phil Stone, beyond the derision of his generation in Oxford, Katherine Anne Porter found it in illness, Walker Percy in a fortunate choice of an uncle.

I have heard of a belief among the Sephardim that for everyone there are twelve teachers, and that at some time in a person's life they will all appear, but they will be disguised. My teachers, my private friends, began to appear early, when life was still autobiography, when they were most needed and least recognized, when neither I nor they knew what they were.

Maybe Stendhal was right to end his autobiography by his twentieth year, before he became a conscious observer and the events of his life, his crises, his lovers, and even his teachers had become guides to the transmutation and the knowledge to write fiction, sources sometimes in gestures, sometimes happening, sometimes told, fonts of those minutes that ring true, echoes of voices, private and universal. I sometimes wonder if for a novelist, autobiography as such doesn't have to stop very early, before lives are transformed into work, or as a thing remembered—or better, recalled, which is different.

Recalled—called back, as if I were there. It is 1928, and I am ten years old, climbing the stairs, something in me climbing those stairs, up and up to the fourth floor, past the stained glass windows on the landings, sun and prism caught, with the smell of wood in an old house and trails of notes from pianos and once in a while a scratchy violin escaping out into the hall.

Like other children of my time I "took" things; taking didn't mean stealing, or catching a disease, or dope. It meant first dancing and then music lessons and then the small, deceptive last, something called elocution. I was lousy at dancing, so I was always put with my best friend, Betty Coopey, who had breasts before anybody else did, in those tableaus made famous by eurythmics where you had to carry big flower wreaths and swoop around touching the tops of them together, hoping to God you wouldn't stumble and embarrass your mother, who hated that sort of thing. They were all the dancing teacher could think to do with us.

Her stars were Betty and Ann, tap dancing like Busby Berkeley girls in shiny sateen costumes, and acrobatic dancing, doing back bends and splits that I could never do. The ballet dancer was Caroline who was almost professional, and I envied her with my soul. We were all at that point about eleven years old. I couldn't have done a back bend or a split to save my life, and my feet were wrong for staggering up on my toes—toes, not points—nobody said points.

My mother said that Betty Coopey had breasts early because she was a Yankee. Betty could play the piano and for all those years we used to buy pink song sheets and sing things like "Willow, Weep for Me," *I cover the waterfront, and look at the stars* . . . and *I've got a right to sing the blues, I've got a right to feel low-down* . . . , and wonder if the boys would ever like us.

I couldn't take piano. My father hated noise so he wouldn't let me. My mother had to find some way to get me out of the house in the afternoons after school, since most of the things you "took" really acted as primitive forms of baby-sitting for parents who wanted to be left alone.

I had what was called an impediment in my speech. My brother said I couldn't talk straight. I couldn't say "l"s or "r"s, and I still can't, which makes me sound a little like they say Swinburne did, who started the camp language of England because he couldn't talk straight either. There was no such thing as speech therapy, but there was elocution. So I took elocution.

Those were the days of climbing slowly up the long oak stairs, feeling more peaceful as I climbed, and letting the little tendrils of music reach me from under the doors.

The house had been built four-square upon a corner lot at the turn of the century. It was of a pale organic-colored brick, like a big square mushroom. There were four floors. In the rooms where the recitals were, two of them with their sliding doors thrown open, there were fireplaces of marble that looked like corned beef. It was said to have been lived in by a German during the First World War, who was a spy and had equipment on the top floor, which was the attic and the servants' quarters. It was a real attic, too, even if it was empty you could tell that—raw floors, bare walls, even the woodwork was just unpainted pine. What the equipment was was not explained. But it made the top floor slightly ominous, except to me.

That was because Mr. Maurice Drew waited for me there, a seventy-five-year-old man with ears that stuck up like a faun's, and wisps of white hair carefully brushed that escaped a little when he was excited and gave him a halo that glowed in the sun of the window. Mr. Drew was one of the famous Drew family. He had been a Shakespearean actor, an Act Tor.

How he had come to ground in the attic of the Mason School of Music I never knew. It was as mysterious as the equipment. Had he been left behind by a showboat? Had he been fired from a road company? At the turn of the century they all came through town and the stars stayed at the Ruffner Hotel which had not yet become as dim as it was in 1930, but local men who owned the town still sat on the front porch and watched the river, and carried flasks they got for Christmas.

Mr. Drew didn't have any money, and he scrounged for pupils in a way that the dancing teachers didn't have to because dancing was ok but you wouldn't be caught dead taking something like elocution.

Mr. Drew's two star pupils were myself and Phillip Caplan, who had a lisp, and whose father said that he didn't think he was wasting his money because if Phillip couldn't be an actor he could always be a lawyer. We were Mr. Drew's advertisements. He trained us in a cute little skit—that's the way he sold it, to the Kiwanis and the Masons and the Elks when the women were invited, a cute little skit. I wore a Dutch costume, with wooden shoes and a wig with long flaxen braids and a cap with pointed ends, and a large blue skirt with a white apron. Phillip wore wooden shoes and a black jacket with big silver buttons and wide blue pants and a black cap with a bill. The skit was called "The Census Taker." We spoke with what we thought were Dutch accents combined with Phillip's lisp, and my impediment.

Mr. Drew always asked permission so nicely, my mother said, the silly old man. She said she didn't give a damn. For some reason she didn't like Mr. Drew much. "He certainly must not have been much good as an actor," she would sniff, "after all I've seen Maude Adams and Nazimova." I, who had already picked up the secret gossip that Nazimova was a lesbian, and a lot of other secret facts, like who the chemistry teacher was in love with, and who drank, and why the librarian had a black eye, said nothing. I loved Mr. Drew and I didn't love my mother as much as I wanted to.

So up the stairs, in a brown hair ribbon, a big one like a bat stuck with a brass pin in my auburn hair, my crowning glory, and horn-rimmed glasses, and one leg slightly shorter than the other which was a constant shame at dancing classes, climbing and climbing and still climbing, almost forever, and at the top was Mr. Drew with his faun's ears, and the biggest secret of all.

There were no Dutch girls then. I would walk in the door, and Mr. Drew would look at me, and speak.

"Stop! Still! You are not Mary Lee Settle. You are Brutus!"

And I was.

"Romans, countrymen and lovers."

Mr. Drew's voice would come from farther and farther away as the toga of Brutus fell across my body. "Remember, this is the noblest Roman of them all."

I would draw myself up to about four feet tall, and speak at last a language that I had thought since I was three years old was an isolated, dim sound within me, not the words, not that, but the honesty, the passion, the life under life, all the answers I thought could never be spoken, secret and an opening at last to something universal, and no longer a lonely sound.

"Be silent that you may hear," and Mr. Drew's voice, from far across the attic, "Aristocratic, tall, ROLLL it out over the dirty throng."

"Believe me for mine honor,"

"Honor, show honor." A stretching of some honor muscles; I could feel it.

"As Caesar loved me, I weep for him,"

"Weep, weep, but not really, let your voice tremble. Don't lose dignity. This is the clue to Brutus's pride before his fall. He didn't say he loved Caesar, he said Caesar loved him..."

"As he was fortunate, I rejoice at it..."

"Let your voice begin to rise toward the climax, and remember your breathing." Voice up and up...

"As he was valiant I honor him."

"Now. Drop your voice, you are angry, you are RIGHT."

"As he was ambitious," voice down.

"Clench your fist. Show your CONTEMPT!"

"I SLEW HIM."

He made me learn Hamlet's speech to the players, "speak the speech I pray you *trrippingly* on the tongue..."

Sometimes he let me be Prince Hal, and there I was, eleven years old, meaning every word I let ROLLL off my tongue, down stage (we had both forgotten long since that we were in an attic at the Mason School of Music). "Take the audience into your confidence. You are a rake, a devil with the ladies, a rebel, a wit, but underneath remember that you have a king in you."

"I know you all, and will awhile uphold the unyoked humor of your idleness, yet herein will I imitate the sun, who doth permit the base contagious clouds to smother up his beauty from the world, that, when he please to be again himself, being wanted he may be more wondered at." Those lines were the protection and the *cri de coeur* of my childhood.

Mr. Drew never gave me a woman's part to play, I think because he knew the men's parts, maybe he had played them, maybe he had wanted to, so I was Hamlet the Dane, and Mercutio, "She is the fairy's midwife, in shape no bigger than an agate stone...," but he never would let me be Macbeth. He said it was bad luck.

Once he took us to his church to perform. It was large, red brick, and Methodist and it was on the West Side, a world away from the East Side and we who went through the West Side to swim in the country-club pool wouldn't have been caught dead there. There were a lot of places like that that were branded into us as we grew, no reason, nothing to inform, except that they were places where you wouldn't be caught dead. I saw a lot of the town you wouldn't be caught dead in with Mr. Drew.

It was on a Sunday evening. I wore my Dutch costume, and Phillip his, to entertain for Mr. Drew at his church supper. It was in a half-basement. There was the smell of chicken and cake, and new-baked bread, and mayonnaise and sun and wind-dried laundered cotton dresses, so it must have been summer.

I stepped out onto the small raised platform that was the stage. It had music stands on it, pushed back. There was a knock. Phillip had used one of the music stands for a door. It nearly fell over. It sounded tinny.

"Who iss dot?"

"I am de census taker."

"Yaaah? Vot you vant?"

We were a big hit. The audience kept on applauding at the cute little children in their Dutch costumes. Mr. Drew had told me what you do when there is a lot of applause.

I stepped forward and stood there alone. Phillip had obviously escaped. I can still feel the space all around me, the pool of silence, still smooth my hands on my Dutch apron, and wait for silence.

Then I spoke, too late to catch Mr. Drew's panicked head-shake, his no, no...

"Romans, countrymen and lovers, hear me for my cause!" I could hear a murmur in the crowd, and I knew what to do with that. I let them have it, proud, imperious, "And be silent that you may hear!" The place was dead quiet.

But I knew as I went on what every actor, Act Tor, experiences. I was laying an egg. I had betrayed myself and Mr. Drew. I had gone public, come out of the attic, out of our secret shared world. At the end there was a little clapping here and there, and some smiles, and Mr. Drew took me home. I cried in the car, but I stopped before my mother saw that.

Things went downhill from there. I had written some poetry and everybody crowed about it; my mother said, "I always knew she would be a writer, like I would have been if I hadn't married."

The poetry was strongly influenced by James Whitcomb Riley, but it was, by my new nature, forced into iambic pentameter. "Aunt MYRtle SHE made CHIFfon PIES, us KIDS we LOOKED with HUNgry EYES." Mr. Drew rewrote it, he called it fixing it, until it wasn't mine any more, and he saw that it was published under my name, my first publication in the West Virginia Review when I was still eleven years old. He had made it into lies. I hadn't said punkin. I had said chiffon pie. I hated pumpkin pie and still do and the editing still rankles.

I swore then and there, standing on the stairs of our house, the only person in history to stand just there just then, and I swore by Almighty God—a phrase of Mr. Jefferson's who we were studying that I particularly liked—that I would never write another line in my whole life.

In the late twenties the one bright outlet in small towns was the newly started Little Theater. At first it was wonderful. There was Shakespeare, and Shaw, and *The Importance of Being Earnest* and *Charley's Aunt*, over and over. When Mr. Ramond Savage, the director, called Mr. Drew and asked if he had a pupil who could be Robin a Page in *The Merry Wives of Windsor*, Mr. Drew sent me. So I sat down in the front left corner of the stage in my medieval costume, with a blue hood, and I played with a top. I can't remember that I had any lines, but I found out then that if you sit down left, totally concentrated on what you are doing, no matter what words are flying over your head, you can steal the scene.

Sara Spencer came back from Vassar where she had studied with Hallie Flannigan, who was the source of the new passion for Little Theaters all over the country. Sara Spencer had huge eyes, and a wonderful voice, the concentration of a devil and, as I found out, the patience of a cruel saint. It was said that she would have gone far, whatever that meant, but she had had polio, and walked with a limp. I couldn't quite reconcile the explanation with the fact that she had come back "home" after seeing the world and going to Vassar, which was my Mecca and my hope. She tended to be a little spiritual, and cared for nothing lower than the angels—I couldn't, for instance imagine her reading *Boots and Her Buddies*.

When I was growing up, high-mindedness was derided in towns like mine, especially by "nice" people, and Sara Spencer was high-minded. She suffered for it. Her detractors, and sometime victims of an iron will and a true belief, said she could walk across the water of the Kanawha River. I loved her in a way that made me want to argue with her, bring her down to my own understanding.

Sara Spencer started a Children's Theater in the same abandoned church that had been made into the Little Theater, the Kanawha Players. I was twelve. I stood on the empty stage of the church and Sara Spencer stood at the back of the dark house. It was, for my first time, a real stage, that smelled like one and had ropes and flies and sandbags, and wings. I was, that night, for her, a Chinese nurse. What the words were I don't remember. I remember being taught to feel bowing like a servant. But the total recall is of standing there alone, with Sara Spencer's voice coming out of the darkness, "Again ... again ... No, Mary Lee, you are not a silly little girl in a costume. You are an amah, a nurse. You are old and tired and responsible, and very, very dignified. Show me all that. Again. Again."

It went on for an hour until it was dark outside and I forgot that I would catch hell when I got home. It was an unforgivable sin to "worry" my parents, who were already worried about money in 1930. "You've got to be her, not just mouth her," Sara Spencer called from the darkness.

Finally I, an aging, dignified Chinese amah, who was responsible, spoke my lines and it was right, true pitch, and I knew it and she knew it, and I went home on the bus after dark, completely happy. That night, with that voice coming out of the darkness, I learned that empathy, in writing or in acting, is what makes a fictional person ring true, and all the facts of life cannot replace it. I hear her voice still, "Again, again." Maybe she taught me to rewrite.

But there were other secrets. I distrust the conventional high-minded memories of sensitive, talented children who only recall the first time they read *Alice in Wonderland*, or heard Mozart, or were first conscious of the high flights of angels. I suspect that they have forgotten that they, too, played doctor and nurse, squashed bugs, wet their pants, and talked dirty.

Every Sunday afternoon I went with my parents to the "club" where my father played golf, and my mother sat by the pool and gossiped, and I lay in the sun hoping for a tan that never came, only freckles. For six weeks in the evening I laid the suggestion carefully that we stop at friends of my parents on the way home. It was easy.

I had found Pierre Louy's *Aphrodite* in the closet of a bachelor brother, and when my mother asked what I was reading I said, "Greek myths." Anyway, that's how I knew about Nazimova, and some other things like, curiously enough, the value of pearls, what you did to get them.

Then I was fourteen, and things were changing and I was getting breasts, too, like Betty Coopey's only not as big, and learning to ballroom dance from a teacher that they said had been trained by Ned Weyburn, not for Busby Berkeley, but for the arms of Fred Astaire. I was being prepared, but not by Mr. Drew and Sara Spencer any longer, or for anything either of them stood for or cared about. It was only lesser girls who went on doing back-bends and splits. When Mr. Drew called to see if I were going to "take" elocution, my mother said I had other interests. I never even thanked him.

Other things were changing, too, and for the worse. Mr. Ramond Savage had gone, and he was replaced by what I see now was the next stage, a faulty one, of the Little Theater movement. Unemployed actors and disappointed directors were taking the local jobs, and they brought with them their longings, their taste,

and their failure. There was no more Shakespeare, no more Shaw; they were replaced by what they called "Broadway plays," as soon as they were released to be printed in French's little books, and we learned to say "sides" instead of "lines," and swanned and swooped and were sophisticated, which was the be-all and end-all in the thirties. I knew, having never in my life been fooled about this, that what we were doing was second-rate.

I was growing, without realizing it, what was called then a veneer of sophistication over innocence without a cushion of any wisdom at all. There was nobody to help me with that. Those years were the arid years, the years of adolescent grief. But I could dance at last, and I had grown tall, and when I left home people said I was "good-looking." When I cut school to go to the picture show, I went every afternoon to the Rialto to see Noel Coward in *The Scoundrel*. I had three records that I played over and over until my parents cried for mercy: Nellie Lutche, Flagstad and Melchoir singing the Liebestodt, and Hal Kemp. What the other songs were I don't remember; it was a sophisticated sound.

I was misspending my youth like a profligate, and when I thought of Shakespeare, I thought, as always, of Prince Hal, who had a king in him. At least I saw it that way.

When the voices intruded, I hated them; I was afraid of being caught listening. I wanted, not to be loved, I didn't see it that way—I wanted to be accepted. I longed to be mediocre and sat dreaming mediocre dreams in the white underwear that my mother said was acceptable, like not wearing your hat at a "cute" angle, or talking topics at a social gathering.

It has taken a long time to thank the tired, patient angels who guided me for those years that I see now were not lost at all. I was hearing and seeing and being, no matter how false it was, a part of things, not outside the gates of mediocracy, knocking to get in. Wisdom had no place in these triumphs and these yearnings, thank God. If I had been wise too early I might have become a critic.

But I had heard the voices and found the words, and found them outside myself. When the voices are shared, and a universal language is recognized in a small world, surrounded by people who don't hear the same words, or find the same possibilities in them, time doesn't matter. It is the same with me as it has always been, beyond taste into what is true, either in pitch or empathy or passion. I have been foolish over most of the decisions of my life, except for that. True pitch is true pitch whether you are six or sixty.

There have been other teachers, other times, but they have come after I grew up and autobiography, as such, stopped. But there are still two voices, and I can call them back when I need them and I do, "Speak the speech I pray you *trippingly* on the tongue," and the voice from the darkness, "Again...again..."

Mary Lee Settle is the author of *The Beulah Quintet* and won the National Book Award for her novel, *Blood Tie*.

A Man Between Nations: The Diary of Peter Pitchlynn 1828 - 1837

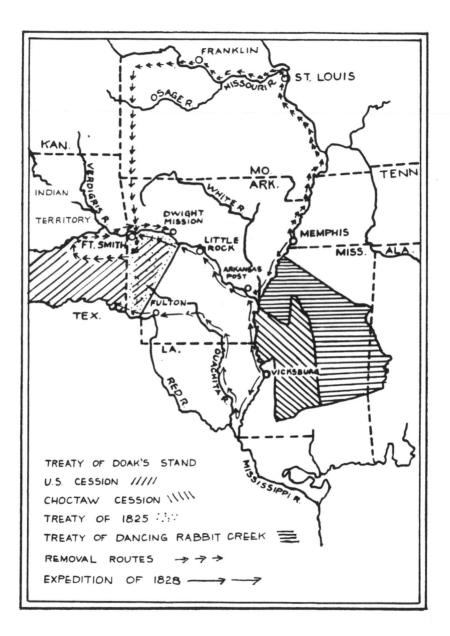

TREATY OF DOAK'S STAND
U.S. CESSION /////
CHOCTAW CESSION \\\\\
TREATY OF 1825 ∴∵∴
TREATY OF DANCING RABBIT CREEK ≡
REMOVAL ROUTES → → →
EXPEDITION OF 1828 ———→ ——→

A Man Between Nations:
The Diary of Peter Pitchlynn

In the iconography of U.S. Government-Native American relations, no event besides the defeat of the Seventh Cavalry at Little
Big Horn has achieved greater importance than the removal of
the Five Civilized Tribes from their homelands in the South. Very
early, the government lighted upon the idea of moving whole
tribes to an area of the country that would not be occupied by
whites—an area which at that time was thought to be a "Great
American Desert." That event has come to symbolize the U.S.
Government's dealings with American Indians.

The Indian removal was not just the "Trail of Tears," an isolated
act victimizing one tribe in the 1830s, but one of the most persistently
followed government policies in U.S. history, covering dozens of
tribes and lasting for almost a century. The motive for removing
the Indians and concentrating them in one wilderness area varied
from the humane hope of maintaining tribal integrity to the blatant
desire to get as much Indian land as possible as cheaply as possible.
Those who either propounded or cooperated with the idea included
not just whites of dissimilar political persuasions but Indians as
well, both fullblood and mixed blood, both established leaders
and rebels. The removal is emblematic of the U.S. attitude and
handling of the American Indians because it was, finally, a wholesale
approach in which intimidation and thinly veiled bribery played an
important role. The actual removal of tribes was characterized, over
and over, by U.S. officials in the field, including Indian agents and
military officials, generally doing their best in impossible situations,
but being frustrated by an almost totally unresponsive government
bureaucracy, leading to situations in which hundreds of people died.

There are government reports, military communiqués, and
descriptions by missionaries encompassing the period of the
removal; however, the diary of the young Choctaw Peter Pitchlynn
may be the only first-hand, on-the-scene account by a member
of one of the tribes. The Choctaws, one of the largest and most
civilized of the great Indian nations, were the first tribe to be
removed en masse to the Indian Territory. Their experience would
serve the government as the example to be followed for all subsequent removals. This diary is particularly interesting because it

directly relates the state of mind, interests, and concerns of a young Indian of prominent family concerning the removal from their homelands in the southeast. Pitchlynn, in fact, would later become for a time the Principal Chief of the Choctaw Tribe.

Pitchlynn's diary is also valuable because the first part of it describes events preceding the removal, including an extended account of the surveying party to the Indian Territory in 1828, during which Pitchlynn pays very close attention to details of topography, game and natural resources. The sequence of events leading up to the removal, and the selling of the idea, are less well known than the dramatic Trail of Tears experience itself, but perhaps ultimately more important, because they provide insights into how and why this policy became realized.

In the first part of the diary we follow the tour organized by the government for the purpose of encouraging the voluntary emigration of the wary Chickasaw and Choctaw and the belligerent Creeks. The Reverend Isaac McCoy, a well known Baptist missionary to the Potawatomi, was a leader of the expedition, but Captain George H. Kennerly of the United States army was in actual command. Lieutenant Washington Hood of the army was its topographer, and George P. Todson its physician (Todson had been cashiered from the army in 1826). All held their appointments from the Secretary of War. Isaac McCoy's *History of Baptist Indian Missions* (Washington and New York, 1840) contains a history of the expedition.

The entire company consisted of thirteen Chickasaws, six Choctaws, and four Creeks, along with various white men serving as interpreters, and a few black slaves. Pitchlynn was one of the delegates of the Northeastern district of the Choctaw. Harper Lovett, the Creek interpreter, died two weeks after the party left Saint Louis. Seven "hired men" or camp helpers were employed at Saint Louis, and the Osage interpreter, Noel Mongrain, joined them at the western line of Missouri. They thus numbered over forty men and, according to McCoy, some sixty horses.

Although the tour did little to advance the removal, it did yield results. The distaste which these Indian farmers and hunters of the southern woodlands conceived for the treeless grasslands of Kansas prepared them to look with less aversion on the wooded land west of Arkansas. Also the meeting of the Choctaw and Osage leaders under friendly official auspices appears to have put an end to the historic animosities between these two important tribes who were soon to be neighbors.

A second part of the diary includes a brief description of Pitchlynn's own entry into the new lands during the winter of 1831-32, when he led a group of five hundred out of Mississippi. Pitchlynn separated from his group, either at Memphis or after a brief time at the Post of Arkansas. He may have been with the small party who took the group's horses on to Little Rock. At any rate, his diary makes no mention of the terrible conditions at the Arkansas Post, where his group along with two thousand other Choctaws endured a blizzard with inadequate food and clothing and almost no shelter. His diary takes up this part of the experience—the removal itself—beginning in late January, 1832, at a point after his separation from his group. His principal goal was to get ahead, survey the area, and find a good place where his own group and his family could settle.

The third part of the diary is an anecdote, occurring five years after settlement in the new land, exemplifying the tensions that were already beginning to arise between white settlers in the Indian Territory—Sooners by about sixty years—and Pawnees. This is a verbatim account of murder and kidnapping and was written down by Pitchlynn on the spot. An interesting aspect of it is Pitchlynn's highly sympathetic attitude toward the whites. He does not think of them as competitors or encroachers but as fellow sufferers at the hands of what he considers to be "hostile" Indian tribes. Conflicts between the tribes would plague the removal period, as the government continued to pen them together in the Indian Territory.

Much later, however, toward the end of Pitchlynn's life, the encroachments of whites on Indian land would worsen considerably, and the period of the removal finally gave way to a new U.S. policy of dissolving the tribes as landholding institutions. This new policy, largely achieved by 1900 in Oklahoma, considerably decreased the total area owned by Indians and made it far easier for whites to divide and then buy them out.

Pitchlynn's diary, then, encompasses the early explorations leading to the removal, the move itself, and, in an ominous coda, an incident concerning one of the dangers that the removed tribes faced five years after arrival.

The story of Peter Pitchlynn's ancestors provides almost a capsule summary of the Choctaws from the mid-eighteenth century on. During this period the tribe's homelands were divided into three districts in central Mississippi. The outcome of the French and Indian War forced France to abandon the American West in 1763, opening up the area to British traders and a few adventurous settlers.

The Choctaws were assimilative. They were town dwellers, living in log cabins with dirt floors and smoke holes in the centers of their roofs. They raised truck patches with melons, beans, potatoes, squash, and pumpkins. Planting and harvesting were communal. From the earliest, the Choctaws welcomed outsiders. Throughout the South among Indians and traders, pidgin Choctaw was the trade language. Choctaws quickly took up skills learned from others, and became particularly good at farming. They had a tradition of mixed-blood leadership, with mixed bloods tending to be among the higher class. Of the Native American tribes, the Choctaws were among the most thrifty, provident, and best governed.

Isaac Pitchlynn was a British trader who travelled to the home of the Choctaws and died of illness, leaving his eighteen-year-old son John (born circa 1756) in the care of the tribe. John settled in the eastern part of the Choctaw homelands, subsequently marrying twice. Sophia Folsom, daughter of another trader, was the second of his two wives. She raised eight children, including Peter, who was the eldest from this marriage and became John's favorite. John ran a trading post on the Tombigee River, five miles north of the present Columbus, Mississippi, at a place locally known as Plymouth Bluff.

After the American Revolution, control over the land north of the Gulf coast was disputed between Spain and the United States. John Pitchlynn acted as an interpreter in the effort by U.S. emissaries to gain trading dominance over the Choctaws, and later he was appointed permanent interpreter. Eventually the Spanish lost out, and in 1801 the Choctaws agreed to a series of treaties that delineated their boundaries and made them dependent on the United States. John Pitchlynn's role expanded, until he was acting as a temporary Indian agent. In 1811, the famed Shawnee orator Tecumseh met the Choctaw near their home, and called upon them to join the Shawnee in opposition to the United States. John Pitchlynn and others opposed him, however, and Tecumseh was unsuccessful—which would become a source of tension between the tribes in the future.

Efforts to move Indians out of their homelands began almost as soon as the Louisiana Purchase was completed, during Thomas Jefferson's presidency. The conclusion of the War of 1812 contributed to a new sense that the nation was destined to grow. Secretary of War John Calhoun decided to aggressively pursue this policy of moving the Native Americans—for his part, probably more in the hope of preserving and civilizing them than stealing their lands. In 1817, he sent a commission to the Choctaws, but not many of them welcomed the proposal. Calhoun later dispatched Andrew Jackson, who had defeated the British in 1812, to press the issue. Some of John Pitchlynn's family were among those who liked the idea, and his oldest son James made the move and declared himself to be chief of the Choctaws in the West. The Principal Chiefs of the tribe refused the offer, despite the fact that some fullbloods did express a desire to move.

In the spring of 1820 Jackson again came and, with John Pitchlynn interpreting, declared that the United States was anxious for the members of the tribe to move to lands west of the Mississippi. When tribal leaders again resisted, Jackson threatened them. Jackson's threats, plus $4,600, five hundred of which went to John Pitchlynn and seventy-five to his son James, turned the tide, and the treaty of Doak's Stand was signed on October 18, 1820.

When it was discovered that lands ceded to the Choctaw tribe included parts of northwestern Arkansas where there were already several white townships, tribal leaders were brought to Washington to secure a new treaty. They were given the first-class treatment while in Washington. Twenty-five hundred dollars was spent on clothes, jewelry, and whiskey. The old chief Pushmataha contacted croup and died, but the Chiefs eventually signed a treaty giving away their Arkansas lands for six thousand dollars annually, designated to be spent on education.

Peter Pitchlynn, called Snapping Turtle by his full-blood friends, was actually only one-quarter Choctaw by blood. He was raised very much as a Choctaw, yet as the son of a well-to-do white trader was always somewhat set apart. In the early 1820s he attended school for about two years; during this time he also helped form a local police force and tried to curtail the whiskey trade in his district.

When a school for boys was set up at Blue Springs, Peter led twenty-one students on the arduous journey across Tennessee to the new school. Soon afterwards, young Pitchlynn became involved in the issue of whether to accept the latest proposal to remove the tribe to the West. This time, the negotiations occurred at the town of Wilson in the Choctaw Nation, where a commission that included General William Clark of Missouri offered the tribe one million dollars to move. Many members of the tribe, including Peter, did not like the proposal and vigorously opposed it.

Deciding that he needed further schooling, Pitchlynn enrolled in the Choctaw Academy for three months but after that brief time quit, went home, and again involved himself in tribal affairs. Thomas McKenney, the first head of the newly organized Bureau of Indian Affairs, met with the tribal leaders in 1827, once again pushing the idea of the removal, and Peter served as a secretary to the proceedings. McKenney failed, but he suggested to the tribe that they send a delegation to the new lands in the West for the purpose of surveying them and seeing for themselves how desirable they were. Whatever his feelings about the removal, the exploration certainly appealed to young Pitchlynn's spirit of adventure.

With financial assistance from McKenney, Pitchlynn first made another effort at improving his education, enrolling in the University of Nashville for six months. Years later, he recalled that he had graduated from there, but as with some of the other claims he made late in life—for example, that he had founded the Lighthorse, ended polygamy in the tribe, and been leader of the 1828 expedition— this wasn't true. His time in Nashville was not wasted, however, for he did buy and read books while he was there.

He then went back to the Choctaw Academy and caused an altercation that ultimately resulted in the Academy being closed. Pitchlynn protested that the school was dirty and in disrepair, the food was inadequate, and the negro servants were disrespectful. In response, the Academy Director, Colonel Richard M. Johnson— a Senator from Kentucky who would be elected Vice-President of the United States in 1836—countercharged that Pitchlynn had himself just wasted five hundred dollars of the tribe's money on his own false attempt at an education. While this controversy still raged, Peter departed on his expedition to the West.

In 1840, during one of his many later journeys to Washington, Peter Pitchlynn met Henry Clay on a steamboat in the Ohio River. The steamboat was delayed, and as was common on those occasions, passengers devised a "mock trial" over the issue of whether the married or the bachelor life was preferable. Pitchlynn was chosen to represent the married and Clay the bachelor side of the question. At first uncertain about what to say, Pitchlynn, remembering Methodist testimonials concerning the religious life, went into a close description of the feelings he experienced as a married man. He did this with gusto, laying particular stress on the goodness of his wife. At the end of the debate, Clay was said to vie with the ladies present at applauding him.

A meeting that occurred on another journey up the Ohio gives us another hint of the personality of Pitchlynn, for he happened to be on the same riverboat with Charles Dickens, who found him very interesting indeed. Dickens wrote of him, in his *American Notes*: "He spoke English perfectly well, though he had not begun to learn the language, he told me, until he was a young man grown. He had read many books; and Scott's poetry appeared to have left a strong impression on his mind: especially the opening of *The Lady of the Lake*.... He appeared to understand correctly all he had read, and whatever fiction had enlisted his sympathy in its belief, had done so keenly and earnestly. I might almost say fiercely....

"He told me that he had been away from his home, west of the Mississippi, seventeen months: and was now returning. He had been chiefly at Washington on some negotiations pending between his Tribe and the government: which were not settled yet (he said in a melancholy way), and he feared never would be: for what could a few poor Indians do against such well-skilled men of business as the whites? He had no love for Washington; tired of towns and cities very soon; and longed for the Forest and the Prairie.

"I asked him what he thought of Congress? He answered, with a smile, that it wanted dignity, in an Indian's eyes.

"He would very much like, he said to see England before he died; and spoke with much interest about the great things to be seen there. When I told him of that chamber in the British Museum wherein are preserved household memorials of a race that ceased to be, thousands of years ago, he was very attentive, and it was not hard to see that he had a reference in his mind to the gradual fading away of his own people."

Pitchlynn would make many other trips to Washington as a representative of the Choctaws, most of them attempts to get the government to meet various promises made in various treaties and agreements. When the Civil War broke out, he had an interview with Lincoln, and they agreed that the best course for the tribe was to remain neutral, despite the fact that Pitchlynn was himself owner of more than one hundred slaves. Although the majority of Choctaws were for the Confederacy, and the tribe split over the issue, Pitchlynn was elected Principal Chief of his people, 1846-66.

Pitchlynn died in 1881, after spending years of his life pursuing Choctaw claims. It would become the general theme of the entire later part of his life. His own later financial and political aspirations were finally so unsuccessful that he died penniless and in debt. Similar stories were played out in the lives of many formerly prosperous Choctaws in the wake of the war. Pitchlynn had to be buried in a public vault pending further arrangements. Yet, during his life he made contributions to Choctaw education, he negotiated treaties, he was the Chief of the Tribe during the Civil War and a National Delegate after 1865. The Supreme Court eventually awarded the tribe three million dollars, but not until Pitchlynn was gone. During his lifetime, he had been suspect by both whites and Indians. He had been a man between nations.

Although the excellent biography of Peter Pitchlynn by David Baird (Oklahoma, 1972) was written before Pitchlynn's diaries were available, we have made reference to it in this foreword and in some footnotes. The diary was in the hands of collector/scholar Lester Hargrett, who had begun the laborious process of deciphering, typing, and making notes. Without his knowledge and work, this version of the diary could not be presented. We have relied in many instances on his notes to illuminate the text.

The diary itself presented an editorial challenge, both because of the inevitable problems of understanding details of the American frontier 165 years ago and because of the shape the diary was in. It is in no way a neat document. Much of it was written literally with a pencil on Peter Pitchlynn's knee in the woods, and entries are sometimes not in serial order. Some of the dates are incorrect, much of the language is rough, repetitive, and a peculiar mix, to the current ear, of the colloquial and the bookish. The editors have chosen silently to correct the spelling of words like "tuck" to "took" and "cold stone" to "coal stone." While something is lost by making such corrections, the overall manuscript is finally more readable. Most importantly, we have made numerous cuts, avoiding passages that are either repetitive or of less interest.

In a word, this is a version of Peter Pitchlynn's diary rather than the thing itself. Scholars should refer to the actual manuscript diary, which is at the University of Oklahoma, in the Western History Collection.

Thanks to Librarian John R. Lovett and Curator Donald DeWitt there for their help with this project.

Speer Morgan
Greg Michalson

-1828-

WHEN WE MADE our departure from our country we knew not what would be the result—whether we should again return to it, or be left to moulder in a foreign land, unburied and unlamented. And notwithstanding our hearts were proud, and cared not for danger, we yet from the aspect of things ahead could not refrain from indulging ourselves in visionary forebodings.

There was before us an extensive, and unknown region, which we were to enter, our road laid through nations that were rude and that loved war, particularly that of the Washashees, with whom we have been for the last forty years upon the bitterest terms of enmity.

Agreeable to the understanding the nation had with Government, we were appointed as Delegates on the part of the Hayeypatoola District to accompany our older brothers the Chickasaws through an exploring expedition to the north, and west of Missouri, and round by the way of the country belonging to the Choctaws west of the Arkansas Territory. According to which, we left the Nation on the 26th of September and proceeded on to Memphis where we fell in with the Chickasaw Delegation. From this place we ascended the Mississippi River in a steam boat for St. Louis and we arrived on the 12th of October after a pleasant voyage, seven days on the river.

We had scarcely landed in the port of St. Louis when General Clark came down and invited the delegations to accompany him to his residence. We did so and were hospitably entertained by him until arrangements were made for our residence during our stay. In this place we had the satisfaction of seeing some of the Sioux, a people but little known to the Choctaws. From every appearance, they seemed to be a poor and miserable race. Their dress and manners were different from any people we had yet seen, and their language bore not the least similarity to that of the Choctaws. They consented to have an interview with us.[1]

We met in the house of General Clark. We stated to them briefly the object of our expedition—that the Choctaws had thought it proper to send us to see the people of other nations of red

---

[1] This incident would presage a generally poor relationship between the Choctaw and the Sioux.

people and hold talks of peace and claim them as their friends and brothers. We had come a long ways and were truly happy to see them. When we returned to our country, we should tell the Choctaws of them and that they should be remembered by our nation and considered in future as our brothers and friends, and that they should not be forgotten if they were far from us. We exhorted them to do the same. By this means our friendship would remain undiminished. We then presented to them tobacco and wampum for their principal chiefs, and also a written talk. After this we shook hands and closed our interview.

The winter being close on hand, the Chickasaws did not think it practical to explore the country recommended by Col. McKenny[2] and after some consultation between them and Clark, it was agreed upon to abandon that intention, and only look at the country west of Missouri and Arkansas. This was also satisfactory to the Choctaws, as we were anxious to get on to our country on the Arkansas and to have that explored thoroughly, so much so at least as to be able to give correct information to the nation of it.

We made our departure from St. Louis on October 18th, and crossed the Missouri River at St. Charles. Our course from this place was generally northwest. After traveling two hundred miles in this direction we crossed again this river. The breadth of this river is three-quarters of a mile. After this, our course was generally the same until we reached the state line and the Shawnee Nation. All the lands we have seen so far belong to the whites, and is settled in places tolerably thick. This country needs no description. It is principally prairie.

We proceeded without delay through St. Charles, Franklin, and several little towns. Arrived at the western line of Missouri without any accident except to the Creek interpreter, who had been unwell previous to our setting out from St. Louis and after several days traveling became so unwell that it was impossible for him to proceed any farther. I have heard since that he died five days afterwards. He was a man of a good mind and excellent disposition, and just in the morning of life, but now lies in a distant land where no parent, brother, or sister ever will see the little mound that wraps him in mouldering clay. He made his journey to that country from whence no traveller returns. His Spirit has gone to seek admission where there are no disputes as to the rights of soil.

---

[2] North of the Missouri River.

We reached the western line on November 2nd, and remained there one week in order to get an Osage interpreter. We however passed the time very agreeably with our older brothers the Chickasaws. The day after we reached the line,[3] we received a visit from the Great Prophet of the Shawanoes,[4] brother of Tecumseh, who fell in a battle against the Americans.

The Prophet appears to be about 50 years of age, of common height, stoutly built and of a commanding appearance. He is blind in the right eye. His dress was more in the fashion of the Chickasaws than of the Choctaws. During our introduction, he exhibited pleasure and sometimes even satisfaction.

On the following day we were visited by Perry and Cornstalk, two of the principal chiefs of the Shawanoes. Perry is a stoutly built personage having a very determined countenance. His dress was simple, consisting of a hunting shirt, cotton leggings, and moccasins of dressed deer skins, handkerchief round his head. The Cornstalk is taller than the Prophet or Perry and of a more serious cast. His dress was very poor, being a common coarse gray frock coat worn out at the elbows and coarse about the skirts.

We spent the day with those chiefs, opening still wider the white path of peace. They returned in the evening,[5] and early the next morning the Prophet and the chiefs came to our camp to have a general talk with us. Perry first rose and spoke for some length of time. He was glad, he said, that we did not pass his nation as strangers, that we had, after travelling a great distance, come to see him. He then spoke some time of the former interviews they had with our forefathers, and that it seemed the Great Father had ordered it so that we should meet again and take each other by the hand. After he had ended his speech he presented to each of

[3] November 4, the day of Andrew Jackson's election. Jackson had been the principal government negotiator attempting to move the Choctaw to the West.

[4] This was the famous Shawnee medicine man Tenskwatawa or The Open Door, who in 1805 had received in a trance the revelations and doctrines which inspired his brother Tecumseh's vision of a great western and southern Indian confederacy. The Prophet and a body of his converts were attacked and defeated by General William H. Harrison at Tippecanoe in 1811, while Tecumseh himself, with the approval of the British, was in the South trying to incite an Indian uprising against the United States—and finding his efforts among the Choctaws defeated by the influence of John Pitchlynn, the diarist's father. After the War of 1812 The Prophet lived in Canada on a British pension until 1826 when he rejoined his tribe in Ohio. In 1827 he moved with his band to Cape Girardeau, Missouri, and in 1828 to the Shawnee reservation in western Kansas, where we are now meeting him, thoroughly chastened. He died in 1837.

[5] "Evening" generally refers to afternoon. The periods of the day were morning, evening, and night.

the delegations white beads and tobacco as a renewer of our old friendship.

The Prophet then rose and spoke some length of time on the subject of the ignorance of the Indians in general. He said that they knew not anything, even that which was good for them. He then spoke of the great wisdom of the President of the United States. He said that he knew what was for their good. Knowing these things to be true, he said that he had given up his own opinion on things respecting the interest of his nation and that he looked to the Great Father, the President, to advise in every thing, and that he obeyed him in all things like an obedient child, and recommended that we should do the same. After closing his speech he presented purple strands of beads and, with it, tobacco. He said this tobacco must be spoken in a council when you return to your country, that the first puff should be in remembrance of the place where we had met them, the second in remembrance of your wives and children, that it was the great duty of man to love and provide for them the comforts of life, and the third should be in remembrance of our older brothers the Shawnees. After this we were invited to visit their town. Evening growing late, they returned home.

On the morning of the following day we started over to their town, which was five miles off. When we got in sight of the Shawanoes we beheld the American flag waving high in the center of their town. They had prepared for us a dinner and we were accommodated soon after we had reached the village. After taking dinner we returned to our camps and bade them farewell. The Shawanoes are situated on the western line of Missouri. In a few years, I think, they will all be tillers of the soil. They have not much game because it is nearly hunted out. Their manners and customs are pretty much as those of the Choctaws with but a few exceptions.

They told us that they had not been there more than eight months and what they had for us to eat at their dinner was what their Great Father gave them, and that they had not anything themselves. We were treated by the Shawanoes with the utmost friendship. They seemed extremely rejoiced at our interview and, to use their own language, we met like long separated brothers. They were all pleased with their new country, and I thought the country was good, but by far inferior to our country here.

November 7th. Rode twelve miles out in the Shawnee lands. Passed through Fithes Town. This place is not quite so eligibly situated as Perry's Town nor are the improvements as good, but the land about it is most excellent, and from information, it is well watered. I proceeded on in a northern direction, travelled about four miles and reached the trading house for the Shawnees and Kansas nation. Saw today the Prophet, shook hands with him for the last time. Killed today two turkey hens. I neglected to place in my book that I killed another deer. Kincaid another. Red Dog also another.

November 9th. The morning with us was busy. Mr. McCoy delivered a short address and prayers after which we soon mounted our horses and set out upon expedition[6] to the Santa Fe Road, crossed it, and continued our course. At length we came to the Blue River after travelling thirteen miles of all prairie, and it very windy and unpleasant. I went hunting after striking camp, and killed nothing but a muskrat.

November 10th, Monday. Owing to not finding our horses early we did not get off soon. Left camp at 9:00, travelled due south until we reached another prong of the Blue. Crossed two more prongs of the Blue, and at length took camp on the waters of the fourth prong. The streams are of rock bottoms. The lands we have passed over today have been high and not very good, but is certainly the best watered country that I have ever seen. There is a great deal of brush on the waters of the Blue.

Crossed today the main Santa Fe road. Travelled only nine miles, went out in the evening and killed three bear. Saw plenty of elk signs, weather pleasant.

November 11th. The lands we travelled over today have been high, rolling beautifully and extending as far as the eye can reach. The lands are not rich, but well watered. The waters of the Blue & Osage nearly reach each other. There is a dividing ridge between them, extending east and west, on which we saw much elk signs but not deer. The company travelled fourteen miles, and I about

---

[6]This was Sunday. McCoy held a prayer service every Sunday. He wanted to dispense with travelling on the Sabbath but "a company of forty men, anxious to get out of the wilderness, few of whom have any religious regard for the Sabbath, cannot be persuaded...to rest for conscience sake." (McCoy p. 354)

---

twenty. This would be the prettiest country in the world if it was only timbered, but it is all prairie.

In my rambles I came to the main Osage River. It is from bank to bank fifty yards wide; a beautiful river. We are now camped on the banks of a small fork of the Osage. I have explored today one of the streams of the Osage. The weather is beautiful and pleasant.

November 12th. We left our encampment on the small creek early in the morning. The weather is cloudy, smoky[7] and cold. We had not proceeded more than two miles when we crossed another small prong of the Osage. The timber on this creek would be fit for no other use than to make fire with. After leaving this branch, we ascended a high hill from which we saw as far as the eye could reach, all prairie, heavens and the earth. The soil of the prairies today has been inferior, but McCoy and some of the whites with us say that it is first rate, and compared it to those in the vicinity of Lexington, Kentucky.

From the highlands we then descended gradually until we reached the main Osage, on which we are now encamped.

November 13th. Left camp a few minutes before 10:00. Crossed the Osage River two hundred yards above our encampment. The river is from 60 to 70 yards wide from bank. The timber on this river is from three-quarters to one-mile wide, consisting of all kinds of oak, hickory, walnut, hackberry, mulberry, sycamore etc. After leaving the river we wound our way upon the high hills that ranged along a mile from the river in a southwest course until we struck another large fork of the Osage River and are at this time encamped on its south side immediately on its banks. The lands here are generally inferior. Thirteen Indians visited our camp—of the Kansas tribe.

November 14th. Started from camp this morning a few minutes before 9 o'clock, the morning cloudy and cold. We travelled up the river on which we encamped and have pursued all day generally a south course. I left the company and made my way up to the top of the high hills and travelled on them for some time. The wind blew strong and cold. As far as I could see to my left the face of the country seemed mountainous. There was a great deal

---

[7] "smoky": foggy.

of lime stone on the sides of those mountains. Soon after I had rejoined the company I heard a gun fire. It was Love,[8] who had shot at a deer. As soon as the gun fired we heard oft nearby a scream. Upon examination it was a woman, of the Kansas tribe. She seemed very much affrighted. I was sorry for her. She was rude and wild in her aspect.[9]

From this scene I left the company again and wound my way among the high hills and valleys. In my route I saw an Indian. My friend Love was with me. The Indian started towards us in a trot as soon as he saw us. He approached us in a pleasing manner and said howdy, and then begged my friend Love for his dog, and then for some tobacco. He was no doubt a husband to the woman who we just had affrighted by our approach. Also a Kansas, his dress consisted only of an old blanket that he wrapped around his shoulders in the Indian fashion, leather leggings and moccasins.

Upon my arrival back with the company, they had camped on the banks of the same stream we were on last night. The lands we have seen today have been sometimes moderately rich. More timber today than usual. The sun has not been seen once today. Cold and with the appearance of snow. Our course has been nearly southwest. Owing to the difficulties in crossing some of the gullies, we made turns in every direction. Travelled sixteen miles. I saw today a high bluff on this creek, which was principally rotten limestone.

November 15th. When we arose this morning we found the weather clear and cold. There was a large frost on the ground. The sun rose full in her might. We left camp at 8:00. Crossed the creek on which we had encamped and then travelled along the edge of the prairie. Then we turned and travelled due south until we struck some of the head waters of the Neosho. The timber here is a quarter of a mile wide. The bottoms are rich, but never can be tended. The lands we have seen today have been poor, stoney and gravelly. The wind has been very high all day. So much so that it was very unpleasant to travel. Cold also. Some aluminum and silex. I have several pieces of rock put away for my own curiosity.

---

[8] Probably Benjamin Love, interpreter for the Chickasaws.

[9] Isaac McCoy describes this episode. The woman was apparently afraid they were enemies of the Kansas tribe.

Peter Pitchlynn

November 16th, Sunday. After prayers we started, and from our last night's encampment we pursued generally a due south course until we came to the Neosho, and down it a few miles made camp. We are situated on the eastern banks of this beautiful stream in a place that is truly romantic. There is in front a wall of solid rock and just behind us the Neosho winds her course. We have a fine pasture for our horses. We are within a few miles of the Osage villages. Mr. Mograine tells me that the meaning of Neosho is good water, "Ne" water, and "osho" good.

He says that it is six days travel to where the buffalo ranges. I killed today an animal that I shall call the prairie badger.[10]

I killed also a prairie hen. This place we have agreed to name the Plains of Marathon. The soil of this little valley is rich. The weather has been pleasant, but owing to the hard winds we had to face yesterday and the fatigues of my watch last night I have been indisposed and unable to enjoy it.

We saw today before us four Indians running with all their might to the patch of woods to our right on the creek. They seemed to be wild. I ascended a mound and beheld the whole country for some distance around, and far away to the west the country rolled off beautifully, and about six miles away I saw a person riding. Stopped at half past four, travelled eighteen miles. Had a long talk with Mr. _____ on the _____.[11] My packhorseman, Tishosho Tushka, is unwell.

November 17th, Monday. We proceeded the next morning down on the left side of the Neosho and pursued generally a south course. The Neosho is a very beautiful stream, about eighty yards from bank to bank. We crossed it just at the agency, which is situated about four hundred yards from the river. The Neosho winds her course to the east and extends up a northwest direction, where we see nothing but the hills and heavens meeting.

---

[10] Probably a species of American badger found only in eastern Kansas.

[11] Probably a long talk with Mr. McCoy about the Bible. McCoy describes such encounters: "Among the [members of the southern delegation] was Peter P. Pitchlynn, a Choctaw; though not a professor of religion, he frequently borrowed my small bible to read, which I afterwards presented to him. I had much interesting conversation with him. At one time he inquired how it happened that Christians differed so much in opinion, when each sect appealed to the Scriptures for proof of its doctrines. I endeavored to account for it satisfactorily to him, by the proneness of man to err; ...man is averse to that which is right, and under the influence of this aversion, because truth is uncongenial with his evil disposition, he mistakes error for truth..." (McCoy, p. 355)

There are at this place upwards of two hundred Osages, whose wigwams I shall not forget to describe. The weather today has been pleasant. Saw nothing but a red prairie wolf, smaller than those in the Choctaw lands.

Upon our arrival the Agency runners were sent out for the principal men of the Osages, saying that our object in coming here was partly to hold with them a talk of importance, to make peace: to put an end to the enmity that has so long existed between them and the Choctaws. The runners (as they are so called in this country) left the agency at half past 4:00 and one of them returned a quarter before 7:00, after running at least forty-five miles. Wonderful for man. Man is more than a horse. Visited in the evening Major Hamtramck, the agent of this nation.

November 18th. This morning walked a few paces up the river and came to a high cliff in which I found a strata of coal stone of two inches breadth that extends along for twenty-five yards. This stone has been tried, and has proven to be good. I have been informed that on the Neosho there are large quantities of alum, in a crystallized state, and that on one of its streams has been found lead in large quantities.

Visited today Mr. Pixley,[12] a missionary who has given me considerable knowledge respecting the Osages, which I shall try to put in my book. Wrote a few words of the Osage language. Read several chapters in the Bible in Genesis and then slept awhile. The manner of Osages in burying the dead is to place them about eighteen inches under ground, covering them over with stone sometimes three or four feet above the level of the earth.

This has been a pleasant day but spent in doing nothing, owing to the non-attendance of the White Hair,[13] whom we are desirous to see and talk with.

November 20th. Our course from the Agency was a little east of south. Proceeded over a rolling country. Came to the White Hair's village. The White Hair's village is situated on the west

---

[12] McCoy reports that the missionary Benton Pixley and the Indian Agent John F. Hamtramck "were at wide variance," partly because the missionary was too demanding and impatient, and too ready to "administer reproof." The missionary was forced to retire by the American Board of Commissioners for Foreign Missions, and the agent "continued in office but a short time."

[13] This is White Hair, the Younger. His portrait was painted by Catlin. ("Annual Report for the Smithsonian," 1955, p. 514)

---

bank of the Neosho a quarter of a mile from the prairie. Soon after our arrival we had a council, and talked with the principal man of the Osages on the subject of making peace. Growing late, we smoked the pipe of peace and then returned to our camps.

The weather cold. At night the wind rose and with it we had some snow that covered the ground.

November 21st. This morning the wind not very high and very cold. At 12:00 we were invited to take dinner with Pretty Bird.[14] He is their great man in war, and the orator in council. His house is a quarter of a mile from the village in an open prairie. Pretty Bird's fare was boiled buffalo which was to me delicious, being the first that I ever ate. The Little Bird spoke and said that what he gave us was such as he ate, and that it was the best he had, if he had better he would have given it us, etc, etc. We then were invited to dine with White Hair. He said what he gave us was the best he had, which was what the Choctaws call Tamfulla, and it was good. I had been wishing for some of it since I left the Nation.[15]

At 2:00 we renewed our talks. Major Colbert first spoke and made a lengthy speech. Then Amulbby. After he finished, the Choctaws spoke again. Red Dog first, and secondly Kincaid, and lastly I made the farewell speech. I interpreted for Red Dog and Kincaid. When we concluded it was dark, half past 7 o'clock. I am much pleased with the Osages. They are larger than any persons of any other nation that I am acquainted with in size of body. They are generally tall and lean in flesh.

PETER P. PITCHLYNN: TALK TO THE OSAGES

I am happy to see you. I have travelled a long road. I first came to St. Louis and there saw General Clark, the great friend of the red man. The Choctaws had seen him before, and they

---

[14] McCoy calls Pretty Bird "Belle Ouizo." (McCoy, pp 355-361) He may be identical with Handsome Bird, whose portrait Catlin painted in 1834.

[15] McCoy reports a contretemps during these peacemaking festivities. Some of the Choctaws apparently requested one of the Osage scalps as a gift. The Osage gave them one and pronounced in a speech that according to custom now the Choctaw, who would soon be their neighbors, were now also their allies in war, having received one of their scalps. "This turn of the affair was as unwelcome as it was unexpected to the Choctaws, who made no reply." (McCoy, p. 358)

were very proud when they saw him. To St. Louis we travelled up the Mississippi River in a boat that went by fire. We were seven days on the river. From that place we travelled towards the west, and without any difficulty, we at length reached the Shawnee Village, near which we spent five days. We talked with them as friends and brothers, smoked together and ate together. From the Shawnees we then turned and have now made our camps on the banks of the Neosho, within the center of your villages, and have for the first time taken you by the hand, and had the pleasure of seeing you in person with my own eyes. It was the wish of my greatest chief and all the head men of the Choctaws that I should see you, and I am really glad that this day has at length come when the Osages and the Choctaws should meet, shake hands and talk to each other. It is a fact that our nations have been at times in enmity with each other, and like men and warriors made the ground red with each other's blood whenever they saw each other. The Choctaws are thought to be the largest nation of red people in the United States and they, like other red men, love war, but we have been told by our Great Father, the President, to be at peace with all nations, and teach our young men how to work, and advise them to pursue the ways of the white man. Believing this to be true and the best way for ourselves and the generation to come, the Choctaws now have laid by everything like war, and wish to be at peace with all nations, and particularly the nations of red people. And now we offer you our hands and with it you have our hearts and friendship. And from this day let us be friends. Let that great light, that shines on all nations never again witness any more of war between the Choctaws and the Osages. Let our paths be in future paths of peace.[16]

November 22nd. Set out this morning from White Hair's village for Fort Gibson at fifteen minutes past 10 o'clock. We proceeded this morning over rolling country and soon struck timber, and

----

[16] Recalling this speech later, Pitchlynn dramatized it, saying that the Osage were showing signs of their ancient enmity for the Choctaw and only a slashing oration by him prevented trouble. ("Peter Pitchlynn," *Atlantic Monthly*, April, 1870") In his biography of Pitchlynn, (Oklahoma, 1972), W. David Baird overcorrects the exaggeration by implying that Pitchlynn made no speech at all. As evidence he cites the fact that McCoy didn't describe any such speech and that McCoy deemed the "civilized and half-civilized Indians as less eloquent than the Western Indians."

crossed a creek that is twenty yards wide. It is called the Beast.[17] The soil today has been middlin good. Travelled twenty-five miles.

November 23rd. Set out this morning at twenty-five minutes past 8:00. The wind rose and it blew all day tremendously. Our eyes suffer very much. Blew off our hats very frequently, and carried them a quarter of a mile before we could overtake them. As we ascended the banks, the country to our left was rolling at a distance. On our right was the timber on the creek. After travelling several miles we crossed again the creek on which we had camped. There we saw a solid bed of the coal stone, which seemed to be of the best quality. At times today we saw no timber on our right or left. From here we entered the Cherokee lands, passing down into a valley where there is a considerable quantity of sandstone. The timber about here is blackjack pin oak. Camped in the evening on the east side of a creek (a tributary of the Neosho.) I went a mile along in its bed and saw quantities of coal stone. In the evening the wind became low.

November 24th. Saw a patch of cane today, the first I have seen since my departure from home, and a fine grove of timber— more than any I have seen since I left the Osages. We passed over the relics of an old Indian town three miles in length and two in breadth, then crossed several tributaries of the Neosho and at length, after dark, reached Shotoes.[18] Travelled thirty-six miles.

November 26th. Started from camp at a few minutes before 8:00, travelled over a mile and reached Union Mission. It rained and the wind blew. In the evening we reached the Creek Agency,[19]

---

[17] Labette Creek, from the French La Bête. The party was apparently travelling down the road from the Osage agency to the Creek agency and Fort Gibson. Fort Gibson, near the present Muskogee, was among the several new military encampments set up to keep the peace in the west and supervise the Removal. Built four years before, it was just inside the territorial boundaries of the later Creek Nation, on the border of the Cherokee Nation, 120 miles upstream on the Arkansas River from Fort Smith. The party is now moving out into thinly inhabited territory. The few settlers here are from small groups of Southeastern Indians who had moved early to the new territory.

[18] This was A. T. Chouteau's Grand Saline trading post at the present town of Salina, Mayes County, Oklahoma.

[19] This is the Western Creek Agency, housed in buildings bought from A. P. Chouteau in 1827.

---

and camped one mile below on the banks of the Verdigris. The country over which we passed today is very broken and rocky.

November 27th. I have today done nothing but confined myself upon my back. I wrote a letter to Father, had my horse shod.

Dear Father

We left our encampment at the Shawnee village on the 8th and proceeded southwest exploring the lands between the Kansas and Osage Nations, and all I can say of that portion of the world is that it is good for nothing and never will be, for it is all prairie and nothing but rock and gravel. A tree in that country is a perfect curiosity. The buffalo is still three hundred miles west of that country, and as to deer we never saw none at all, nor any kind of game whatever. The land is generally poor. Notwithstanding that these things are all true, the white people with us have been presumptuous enough to tell us that it is a fine country.

We saw the Kansas Indians, and I know you never saw such people in your life. Their manners and action are wild in the extreme. They are in a perfect state of nature and would be a curiosity to any civilized man. Their dress consists only of leather leggins, moccasins, and a buffalo robe wrapped around their body. Their heads are trimmed close all over except on the back, where a small patch is left and plaited into two pieces. The women also had on leggins and moccasins and nothing more about them than a buffalo robe. Their hair is left to grow long and hang promiscuously over their shoulders. It is said they go perfectly naked in the summer. The Kansas Indians are no doubt a part of the Osages, as they speak the same language.

Without giving you a journal of our travels, I shall tell you something about the Osages. Upon our arrival at their agency we found nobody but a few old men and women. The warriors and principal men were all out hunting, but immediately runners were sent and before twelve o'clock the next day several of them came in, White Hair excepted, who is their Principal Chief. We waited for him two days. At length the company concluded to proceed down to his village, and just as we reached his place of residence, he also arrived and soon we commenced our talk. Before sun set we made a white road and buried forever the tomahawk. At night the wind blew tremendously. With it came snow and by the morning the ground was covered, a white road sure enough, but we spent another day with them, talking and eating.

Peace and harmony will be between the Choctaws and Osages

in the future. One of the most influential characters of the Osages have come with us and is with us now, but he will return back home from here.[20] He is called Pretty Bird and is the greatest man by nature the Osages have. He is their principal man in war, and in council he is their orator. He is truly a great man. From the Osages we travelled south, coming through part of the Cherokee lands, and at length have reached the Creek Agents on the Verdigris. We are five miles above Fort Gibson and sixty above Fort Smith. We expect to be here two or three days to recruit our horses, and then will strike for the Canadian.

I have enjoyed very good health, and I do wish you not to feel the least uneasy about me. Tell mother that I came very near getting married to a half-breed Osage, a very pretty young woman and that I am yet in love with very strongly.

I do not expect to go home with the company. I shall stay behind and go home by water. You must not expect me before March. Kincaid will get home probably in January. You must tell his family all the news I have written. He has enjoyed good health without a day's exception. Present my love to Mother, Brothers, and Sisters, and to all who may inquire after me.

Peter

November 28th. Spent the day principally in writing. In the evening I visited the Creek camps and saw them dance. I am extremely sorry to find people of my own color (Indians) so full of vice as I have found the Creeks are. There is no distinction between them and the Negroes within themselves. They mingle together in society upon terms of equality. There are among them a great many mixed breeds and some of them are influential characters.[21] The Negro men, it seemed to me, were the head managers of the dance. In fact, I have seen no Indian men dancing. They were Negro men and Indian women. Two hundred thirty Creeks arrived today from the old Nation, and have just crossed the Verdigris and are camped on the opposite banks. Colonel Brearly[22] is their Agent. The women of the Creeks are very lewd.

---

[20] Pretty Bird left the party December 1 to return home.

[21] Disagreement about the relative social status of Negroes was an ongoing problem between the Five Tribes, with the Creeks and Seminoles typically either making fewer distinctions or allowing the Negroes more authority than was typically deemed proper by Choctaws and Cherokees. The Creeks were sometimes called "The Breeds" because of their apparent high level of intermarriage.

[22] Colonel David Brearly was agent for the emigrating Creeks from 1826 through June, 1829.

November 29th. I did not get up very well this morning, and I yet feel not so very well. Mr. Richard Fields of the Cherokees (Old Nation) came to my camp, and we have become acquainted. He is a half-breed, and is quite intelligent and a young man of steady habits. He seems to have strong feelings of attachment for his old country, and have not that sanguine opinion of the new country I find with many of the Creeks. I find the Creeks generally pleased with the country. The Verdigris here is about one hundred twenty yards wide, with tolerably high banks on both sides. There is more timber here than I have seen since I left the Shawnees. I have been told that between this river and the Arkansas, the Creek lands are pretty good. Prairies not so large as those the way we came. Since we have been here, the weather has been good.

Major Colbert's horse being lost, we are detained, and have not left here today.

At sundown I got on my horse and rode over to the Creek village, where they were dancing. I joined with them in three reels and then came off. Just upon my arrival, an old woman died within twenty steps of the place where they had made arrangements to have the dance, owing to which the party moved their dance three hundred yards away. This proves that these people are so full of vice that they regard not the death of their nearest neighbor. The dance was carried on near where McIntosh[23] resides.

November 30th. Owing to my ramble last night over to the Creek village, I feel drowsy this morning, yet am well. The sun rose this morning beautifully, and the weather is really very pleasant. Everything seems to rejoice. The birds are singing their harmonious notes, the heavens are without a threat of a cloud. This morning Pretty Bird came to my tent and took with me breakfast, after which we were requested to go to the Reverend Dr. McCoy's tent to receive the benefits of a prayer. At 10:00 we set out from camp and took the road to the fort, crossing a beautiful creek, near which some new cabins had been erected by the Creeks. The lands between the Creek agency and Fort Gibson is good in places.

After crossing the river we went down by the fort and camped below it a mile and a half. I went out in the evening and took

---

[23] The newly arrived Creeks were Chilly McIntosh's followers. The Creek members of the exploring party would remain here with the McIntosh group of fellow tribesmen, then depart back to the East with a letter from McIntosh inviting those still in the East to come to the new country.

a hunt. I had not gone far when I was compelled to forsake my course on account of a large lake. I crossed at where it made a neck on a log, and went down several miles. By this time dark was approaching. I hurried to get back but met difficulties in the cane and bushes.[24] However I took everything patiently and pursued my course towards camp. I reached camp at 9:00. The company laughed at me and said I was lost. There is here plenty of cane. It is only three and a half miles between the mouth of the Neosho and the Verdigris. The lands about here are rich, the timber in abundance.

December 1st. This day has been spent by me in an idle way. The only thing I have done is go up to the garrison and get me two bottles of liquor. Slept and thought of my friends at home. Little wind stirring. Weather pleasant. Just at sunset I loaded up my gun and stepped out, and before I had gone two hundred yards I saw a prairie wolf, which I shot and killed—the second that I have killed in this country. Pretty Bird, the Osage chief, left us and returned home today. I made a short address at his departure.

December 2nd. We left camp at 9:00 and proceeded for the Canadian. The morning was windy and cloudy, much of the appearance of rain. We travelled from camp a southwest course and went through a large cane brake, say two miles in breadth before we reached the Arkansas. The cane here is not large, such as on the Tombigbee, but thick. We forded the river. The Arkansas is a quarter of a mile in breadth, with sandy banks, and bottom. The water is turbid. Soon after crossing we entered the prairie where the wind blew intolerably high—the country was rolling, and at a distance to our left we saw high hills covered with timber in places. The soil in some places was middlin good. This country is too scarce of timber to be inviting. Killed another prairie wolf, and one turkey. Kincaid also killed a turkey. At 12:00 in the night came on a shower of rain and continued raining till day.

---

[24] The Arkansas bottoms were wide here and the switch cane extraordinarily thick. This small cane was about half the size of the sometimes twenty-foot tall giant Southern cane that grew on the Tombigbee River in Mississippi. The frequency with which Pitchlynn notes the presence or absence of cane reflects its importance in the economy of the Southeastern Indians. It was employed in making baskets, mats, furniture, and shelters, among many other uses, as well as providing winter protection and forage for livestock.

December 3rd. The weather cold and cloudy. The soil in no place today was good. Camped on the banks of the north fork of the Canadian. To our right we saw mountains, robed with scrubby timber. The waters we see in this country generally turbid. Saw today buffalo sign. Killed a large buck. Duncan and McTish bantered me and Kincaid that they could kill more game than we could. The bet was a bottle of wine, which we won. I hauled out today my bottle of whiskey, and Kincaid and I drank a health to our friends at home.

December 5th. I got separated from the company and was alone. I travelled till night, struck camp, and just as I laid down I heard guns at camp. I started out and first came to a Cherokee camp and got one of them to pilot me to our camp. Twas after 9:00 when I got to camp. I saw today no good lands. The country is mountainous.

December 6th. Kincaid and myself started together and got on buffalo sign and followed them into the mountains, and by some way we became separated, and I have ever since been trying to get on the trail of the company, but have not. I am now camped on the banks of the Canadian, got poor Sambo tied to a tree, but he has plenty cane by him, and will do well enough. I saw no buffalo, but some bear sign.

December 7th. During last night the weather became clear and cold. Stars decorated the heavens. Sometime before day it again became cloudy, and great appearance of rain. At daylight I again mounted my horse, and pursued my way back the way I came. About 8:00 I came on the trail of my company, having passed over it somehow yesterday. I pursued all day before I got up with the company. The Choctaw lands are generally poor and unfit for cultivation, no springs. The timber principally post oak and blackjack.[25]

I was sorry when I came up with my company to find that

---

[25] The splitting up of the party is the occasion for Pitchlynn's summary comments on the two leaders. In his official report, McCoy states that after having been in the new Choctaw country for only two days, the parties were now splitting up. The two Southern delegations were expected at that time to proceed to Fort Smith, but some of them wanted to remain a while longer to hunt and better acquaint themselves with the country. Captain Kennerly, Lieutenant Hood, Mr. Bell, Dr. Todson and McCoy proceeded back through Fort Gibson and reached St. Louis on the 24th of December.

our leader, Captain Kennerly, had left us. He is in my opinion a gentleman. His conduct towards the delegations has been that which I would expect from a man of good principles and right opinions. Mr. McCoy is a missionary to the Potawattomies and has been leader to our parties, but he is, upon examination, rather superficial in his opinion of things. It seems to be his object to concentrate all the Indian nations within the limits of the United States over on the western side of the Mississippi.

December 9th. We reached this morning the Choctaw agency at about 10:00, and camped by it. In the evening we visited the agent and had a talk. Weather cloudy and drizzling rain. I had the pleasure this morning of seeing my Uncle Edmund Folsom[26] and his son Peter, who I am as proud to see as any person in all my acquaintance. Peter has made considerable improvement and speaks good English. The agent has a healthy looking situation for his residence, but not rich.

December 10th. The first thing I did this morning was write a letter to Father. Took breakfast with Major McClellan[27] after which we left his place and travelled on for Fort Smith on the river on our way to which we crossed the Poteau River on which are valuable lands, in my opinion. The company passed by the fort and have camped a mile below it. This fort is vacant and rapidly on the way to destruction.[28] It is situated on the eastern banks of a rugged bluff, immediately at the mouth of the Poteau. This place is undoubtedly a very sickly place. Around there I see Cherokees, Creeks and a Choctaw drinking. The weather cloudy and warm.

December 11th. I was sorry this morning my friend and uncle Kincaid left me and has gone home. I am now in a manner alone except my friend—is here with me. L—this morning got drunk and commenced a quarrel with me.[29] I am sorry also at parting with my Chickasaw friends and brothers. They left here a few

---

[26] Edmund Folsom the elder, Pitchlynn's great-uncle, had apparently moved west with the early group.

[27] William McClellan, the Choctaw Agent.

[28] Fort Smith was established in 1817 and occupied until Fort Gibson was built in 1824. No troops were stationed there between 1824 and 1833. The abandoned stockade-style fort stood near the confluence of the Arkansas and Poteau Rivers, within sight of the new Choctaw lands.

[29] The friend is apparently Garland Lincecum.

minutes before Captain Kincaid. I looked at the guns and brass kettles at this place intended for the Choctaws that may immigrate to this country. I was invited by my relation Mr. Smith[30] to visit Capt. John Rogers, Chief to the Cherokees,[31] whom I am now with. I find him an intelligent man with a strong mind.

December 12th. Left Captain Rogers this morning and crossed over back the Arkansas in company with my cousin Mr. Smith and Garland Lincecum. Stayed a few minutes at Fort Smith. Went down to Mr. Morse's a few hundred yards below the fort on the banks of the river, and was introduced to the landlady and her daughter, a pert little girl and right pretty too. From thence we went up to Uncle Folsom's place and stayed all night with him.

December 13th. Uncle Folsom and his son Peter, Garland Lincecum, and myself set out this morning for the Choctaw Agency. When we came to the Poteau we found her rising and already unfordable. We went to where there was a ferry and crossed. A mountain to our left called the Sugar Loaf projected up into the clouds, wrapped in a blue mist that gave it a dreary and mournful appearance. It was ten miles off. We reached the agents at about 3:00.

December 14th. Returned to the Fort again, where I have met Mr. Smith. He and I went to a place where some Cherokees were dancing. While I was there, I was promised a wife. I did not accept her. In the night the weather cleared off and a heavy frost fell.

December 17th. Took dinner with Capt. Dodge[32] and proceeded on to Uncle Folsom's, reaching there at sunset. The weather this evening has turned quite cool. Some appearance of snow. Saw some very good lands on the Cherokee side.[33] Old Mr. Rogers'

---

[30] Pitchlynn's mother had at least two sisters and one of them may have married a Smith. In that event, this Mr. Smith, who was probably a white man, would be Pitchlynn's first cousin.

[31] Rogers had come to the west with the first of the Cherokee in 1817; he died in Washington in 1846.

[32] Israel Dodge, a blacksmith for the benefit of the Choctaws, was among the agency or fort employees.

[33] Travelling southwest out of Fort Smith, one entered the Choctaw lands; northwest, the Cherokee.

place is twelve miles above the fort, and is situated immediately on a bluff on the Arkansas River. He has rich lands about where he lives.

There are signs here of an old field. From accounts French traders once lived here.

December 19th. Peter and the old Choctaw and I and some Delaware started today with a gang of dogs into the fork of the Poteau, a bear hunting.[34] After rambling nearly all day in the thick cane, we got home much wearied, but with no game. In the morning I started back to Ft. Smith and on my way I found three deer and killed them. Upon examination, they were all pet deer.

December 20th. Confined all day in bed with the dysentery, with which I was very unwell. Did nothing but read a letter.

December 23rd. In the evening the old Choctaw sent me word to go and see him. I did so, and we had a long talk about the Delawares. He said that the Delaware wished to remain this winter and next summer on the Choctaw lands and that he was much opposed to such a thing. I told him that it was also against my will and that I would if possible have them removed. We finished our talk at sunset and I returned home to Folsom's.

December 24th. Received an invitation from Capt. Dodge to attend at his house a ball to be held on the evening. Uncle Edmund, Peter and I started to it, got there at sunset. I partook in it with some degree of satisfaction.

December 25th. On this day, was it that the Saviour of mankind was born? A day held sacred by all who feel the love of him, and why is it that the day is spent in dissipation, when everyone ought to commemorate it in the most solemn manner.

O how things are changed, from good to bad.

This day I have spent in lounging and resting, for I slept scarcely any last night.

The manners of the people in this country are to me more

---

[34] Small bands of Delaware hunters had for years roamed at will over the present Oklahoma, but the immigrant tribes objected to the depletion of their dwindling supply of game, and by 1835 most of the Delaware had been gathered on a reservation in Kansas. The "Old Choctaw" is not identified.

uncivilized than among the Choctaws. People go to balls without being invited. No regularity in dancing. Everything was dissipation and rowdiness. Among all the girls I did not see but one who had anything like manners about her.[35]

January 4th, 1829. We left Fort Smith today, the weather very pleasant and agreeable. Uncle Folsom accompanied Peter and me out from the fort ten miles and returned back home. We proceeded on together to the Little Rock.

January 5th. Proceeded on, the weather remarkably pleasant. In our course today we had mountains to our right. Came into piny timbered country. Stayed all night with Mrs. Saddlers, who is indeed a fine woman. Travelled today thirty miles.

January 6th. We made an early start this morning and came on pretty rapidly. Let me not forget to mention that Mrs. Saddlers lives on the banks of the Short Mountain Creek, and has a ferry. The mountains to our right all day, robed with green pine. Nothing has pleased my fancy more than the appearance of the mountains. They seemed to possess a magical sight.[36]

After crossing Shoal Creek, we crossed soon after another creek and after leaving its swamp we took a blazed way that led us to Witt's Ferry. We immediately entered piney timbered country, and oh how sweet it was, the winds softly sighing through the boughs of the pines.[37] It touched my finer feelings and brought my imagination into a thousand romantic, etc. We crossed the river, and then reached the mission at Dwight Station at sunset. Distance today thirty miles. Some appearance of falling weather.

January 7th. This morning when I got up it was cloudy. At 10:00 there came a small drizzling rain. I went to the male school and after hearing lessons from them, made to them a short address. Borrowed ten dollars from Washburn. Took dinner with Mr. Wisner. Then came to Hitchcock's room and wrote a letter to Uncle Folsom.

[35] Fort Smith would retain the image of a rowdy, fun-loving, and bibulous place, both as a military emplacement and town, throughout the nineteenth century.

[36] Pitchlynn was travelling along the base of the great southern wall of the Arkansas River valley, a series of peaks dominated by the huge bulk of Magazine Mountain, the highest elevation in Arkansas and a conspicuous land mass. Nuttall had described it as "a magnificent empurpled mountain."

[37] Pitchlynn is obviously reminded of home.

January 17th. Reached today the Post of Arkansas.[38] Distance twenty-seven miles. Country level. Prairie. Struck the woods within four miles of the town.

January 18th. I am at this time on the banks of the Mississippi waiting in great anxiety for a passage. It is probable I shall get off today. I shall soon be striding once more over the lovely hills and plains of the Choctaws, where I long to be. It is now almost four months since I took leave from home, and during that time I have not had the pleasure but once of hearing from my relations and friends. I have naturally a stronger affection towards my relations, and especially for my parents. I have had many a melancholy hour on their account, as I know they have grieved much at my being separated from them.

From the Post we proceeded down as far as Mr. Gondon's, nine miles below, came to this place in a carriage, paid the driver $4.

January 19th. Bought a skiff. Paid $5 for it, and $2 more to an old Spaniard to row us down. We took the Arkansas to the cut off, thence into the White River, and down that river to a cut off again, passing from the Mississippi into the White River, but it is now dry. Left our vessel and took up by land, to Mr. Montgomery. Reached there late in the evening. Saw a Kentucky fight,[39] the first I have ever seen. This has been a day full of scenery.

January 20th. Spent this day in impatience, on account of no boats coming down.

January 21st. This morning the *Car of Commerce* arrived, and we embarked. Sailed all day without any accidents.

---

[38] Arkansas Post was the first white settlement in the lower Mississippi Valley; Tonty, a lieutenant of LaSalle, had founded a trading post there in 1686. It was located about seventy-three miles southeast of Little Rock. In November, 1832, Washington Irving stopped there briefly and found it to be a "decayed, ruinous place."

Little Rock at this time was the capital and the only incorporated city in Arkansas. It was a town of several hundred inhabitants with something over one hundred buildings. The era of steamboats had been going for a decade and about one boat a week hazarded the journey to Little Rock.

Thomas Nuttall reported that "all inhabitants beyond Arkansas Post could be classed only as renegades fleeing from society." Another traveller stated flatly in 1826 that the citizens of Little Rock were "the dregs of Kentucky, Georgia, and Louisiana."

[39] A style of wrestling in which opponents begin by facing each other and grasping the other with both arms around the body.

January 22nd. This morning just at 1:00 we struck a sand bar, and there stuck fast all day.

January 24th. Peter P. Pitchlynn to "Dear Uncle"[40]

Dear Uncle,

We have just reached Jackson, and we shall have the infinite satisfaction in a few more days of striding once more over the lovely hills and plains of our native country. Never in my life have I been so much put to the test of hardship and trouble as I have been since my departure from Fort Smith. While there I was unfortunate, out of money, and dependent on the generosity of strangers. However, I have got through pretty well, but very sick of traveling, and in a prodigious humor for home. The first setback we got was at Witt's Ferry. The ferry man would not put us over because we had not money, and so I had to commence to preach to the damn rascal, which made the thing worse, and at last I had to give him my handkerchief (the only one I had) before he would consent to cross us. That evening we reached Dwight, the Missionary Station. We found them extremely polite and friendly to us, and loaned me ten dollars, which helped us considerable, for which I am a thousand times thankful to them. We spent a day with them. The time passed off very agreeably, for we were among people that were pretty much like us—the Cherokees who were there at school.

-1832-

January 27th.[41] Left David Pickens this morning with the intention of taking an exploring expedition up the Arkansas as far as the Pheasant Bluff. The bottoms of the Poteau are in many places

---

[40] The "uncle" in this letter is probably Edmund Folsom, from whom Pitchlynn had parted at Fort Smith on January 4.

[41] It is three years since the exploring expedition. Since then, Pitchlynn aligned himself with the forces against removal, and was elected a chief of the Northeastern District on the platform of opposing removal. However, President Jackson refused to recognize the new chiefs and forced them to step down. After a series of maneuvers by the War Department, opposition to removal finally collapsed. By October of 1831, 4,000 Choctaws began to gather in their districts for the more than five hundred mile journey.

The decision was made to separate the groups so that no single place would get too crowded.

The removal was cursed by the worst blizzard in memory in the Southwest. Because of conflicting directives, a total of 2,500 Choctaws ended up deposited at Arkansas Post

---

high and dry, beautifully situated for farming, and well timbered—
Spanish oak, hickory of all kinds, hackberry, walnut, puckcorn,
and spicewood are the principal growth of the bottoms on this
river. This bottom lies between the Arkansas and Poteau, and is
at its greatest width about four miles wide and gets narrower until
it comes to a point at the junction of the two rivers a few paces
above Fort Smith. There are within this place valuable tracts of
land, but the misfortune is that there are no eligible places for
buildings, and that it would be sickly to live between those rivers.
For corn and all kinds of vegetables there are no better lands in
the world than those which I have seen today on the Poteau, and
it said to be excellent also for cotton.

I walked this evening down to the bottoms on the Arkansas
River with Col. McClellan and his nephew Mr. John McClellan and
viewed the situation of the lands. The bottoms are fully one mile
from this place and exceedingly rich and well situated for farming
and with heavy timber. The weather clear. Cold south winds. Mr.
Moore is away from home, but I am hospitably accommodated by
his lady and family.

January 28th. Along the edge of the bottom there are several
places that would be fine to settle on—particularly at the Bear's

---

instead of going on to Little Rock as the original instructions had specified. Captain Brown
at Arkansas Post had only sixty tents, and the Indians were forced to huddle together
in open camps and suffer through the bitter cold of the storm. The supply of food was
inadequate. Captain Brown wrote, "This unexpected cold weather must produce much
human suffering. Our poor emigrants, many of them quite naked, and without much
shelter, must suffer, it is impossible to do otherwise; and my great fears are that many
of them will get frosted." There were few blankets, shoes, or winter clothes available.
Most of the children were barefoot and naked in zero-degree weather.

Removal officials, trying to alleviate these conditions, took many emigrants overland the
350 miles to their destination. The roads were in bad shape, and travel was slow, fifteen
miles being considered a "good day." The weather continued to curse the group, with
rain nearly every day in February, exacerbating the condition of the roads. Five months
after the first groups gathered in Mississippi, the removal was finally completed, with
emigrants sick, exhausted, and discouraged. All on-the-scene accounts praised the actions
of the removal agents themselves, who acted with resourcefulness and compassion, doing
their best in nearly impossible circumstances.

Pitchlynn's party, about five hundred in number, went by wagon to Memphis, thence
by the steamer *Brandywine* to the mouth of the White River, thence to Arkansas Post,
and, finally, in late January, on to Fort Smith by the steamer *Reindeer*. Pitchlynn himself
reached Fort Smith ahead of the main party. He had either left the main party after
crossing the river in Memphis or left them after remaining a while at Arkansas Post. If he
left them at Memphis, he was going overland with the group taking the party's horses,
which reached Little Rock two days ahead of the main party. At the time of these entries,
Pitchlynn is moving on to the new lands to explore and select prime locations for himself
and his family, whom he had left in Mississippi until the situation was better settled.

Bluff—This would be indeed a beautiful place if it was not for the little mounds[42] that are stuck here and there on it and disfigure it pretty much. Water by digging can no doubt be got here at no considerable distance below—in fact Mr. Moore informed me that there was a hole of standing water within two hundred yards of the place. The prairies were, I thought, second-rate land but no doubt will produce well. I saw several licks in the prairie, and there was to be seen in them a scum of salt that appeared very white, pretty much as though meals had been thrown on them. The Casue, where we crossed, was about twenty yards from bank to bank and of a rock bottom. In crossing it, my horse fell two or three times on account of the ice on it. I jumped from off my horse onto the bank and got over without being much wet, but it was with some difficulty that my horse got out.

Saw a gang of turkey today. Shot and killed one, but did not get it. I also shot at a deer and wounded it pretty bad. I also shot at an eagle and at the crack of the gun I saw the feathers fly. I am now encamped in the bottoms of the San Bois by the edge of a cane brake where my horses are faring well. I am seated by a very comfortable fire, and have taken my snack of hunting fare, and do think myself happy, notwithstanding I am now fully six hundred miles from home, and in a wilderness where no one has yet made his abode, and with nothing to be seen but interminable cane brakes, extensive prairies, lofty mountains, with their shaggy tops extending above the clouds, and nothing to be heard but the scream of the night owl and the wolf's long lonesome howl. I could write more, but it is now late and I will lie down and take my rest.

January 29th, 1832. I awoke, got up this morning an hour and a half before day; after recruiting my fire, I commenced singing and whistling, as I generally do of mornings, but I did not feel as

---

[42] One of the principal areas of settlement for the immigrants, in and around the current Spiro, Oklahoma, would prove to be the home of some of the most important mounds in North America. The Spiro mounds, near the Arkansas River, housed an astonishing hoard of jewelry, clothing, baskets, and other sophisticated crafts, testifying to a vast system of trade reaching to the Gulf Coast among Native Americans about eight hundred fifty years ago.

The new Choctaw settlement there was called "Skullyville," after the Choctaw word for "money," and Pitchlynn and many others would settle in its vicinity.

Interestingly, mounds figured prominently in at least one version of the Choctaw's creation myth. Another well-known burial mound site in Mississippi, Nanih Waiya, was thought of as "the mother of all Choctaws."

merry as I was when my friend and brother R.M. Jones was with me. My mind, in spite of everything, would turn towards home. I thought of my wife, then came the children, each one in turn.[43] I thought of everything around my long abandoned home. I have certainly thought more of my wife and children this day than any day since I left home. The sun rose this morning in all its splendor and beauty, but it was soon eclipsed by clouds, and the prospect of the day became somewhat gloomy and uncheering. The wind blew from the north raw and cold (as they say in this country) and continued so until evening—the wind has ceased, but there are no stars to be seen and the weather seems as though we shall either have rain or snow.

After taking a hearty breakfast, we caught our horses and made a start about an hour after sunup, and pursued a southwest course to the San Bois Bluff, which I guessed to be about three hundred feet high. From this lofty place I had an extensive view of the country in every direction. I saw the Sugar Loaf Mountain, extending her peaked top high into the element and the Cavernole stretched along to the south like a heavy cloud on a summer's day. To the west I could see the wide spreading prairies, and far off mountains that barely lifted their heads above the intervening hills. To the northeast we saw the Arkansas and its sand beaches and, far beyond her, mountains and prairies as far as the eye could reach, but what interested me more than all these, was the great bottoms on the Arkansas, which I could see above and below for a great distance, particularly those between the San Bois and Pheasant Bluff.[44]

After looking about and around this place, I went down along the edge of the bottoms and took up camp in the edge of the cane—here I had some difficulty in getting wood and water. Broke my knife in perforating a hole through the ice to get water in a creek. Had turkey for supper. The wolves howled within a hundred yards of my camp all night. Had serious reflections. Dreamt about my wife and children. Killed two turkeys.

January 30th, 1832. Got up this morning an hour before day, prepared breakfast roasted a turkey—after eating, took a walk

---

[43] Pitchlynn, now married with two children, would bring his family from Mississippi to the new lands in the fall of that year.

[44] This area would attract a number of Choctaw families. Pheasant Bluff was one of the first trading points in the Choctaw Nation. It was located about seventeen miles northeast of Stigler, in Haskell County.

---

into the bottom. Viewed the lands. Got our horses and started back for Moore's. My birthday...

At the three forks saw the cane in abundance, and very fine tracts of land, enough for fifty or more families to live on. This is about fifty miles from the agency. Timber good, consisting of black oak, post oak and pretty much as those that grow on the Arkansas Pine at the heads of those streams and on the mountains. Water in the San Bois all year. Deer scarce, buffalo range along here sometimes. Bee trees here are in great abundance. Turkeys are very plentiful at the three forks. Some bear.

-1837-

September 23, 1837. We left Rush Creek camp[45] yesterday morning at about 7:00 and proceeded on our route westward—and encamped in the point of timber that made into this prairie which we have named Buffalo Prairie. It is the first large prairie after leaving Washita Prairie. The road runs along on the dividing ridge between the Red and Washita rivers and is a crooked route, but the only one that can be traveled well—for on either side it is a rough and brushy country. We had some very grand views of the country on both sides of the road from the high knobs on the ridge. On arriving here, we found a camp of whites, and to us an interesting one. They had been prisoners among the Pawnees—a young woman about twenty-one years of age and her infant and two little brothers—one about nine years old and the other about seven. Fortunately they had been bought by Mr. Spaulding and were on their way home under his protection. We asked the young lady many questions respecting her captivity and her narrative was as follows:

---

[45] This hunting-trip incident occurred five years after removal. Rush Creek was in the newly created Chickasaw Nation, near Paul's Valley, to the west of the Choctaw Nation. Pitchlynn himself was among the Choctaw counsellors who signed the document within this same year (1837) ceding western lands of the Choctaw Nation to the immigrating Chickasaws.

There were numerous conflicts between the Pawnee and the Choctaw within the new Choctaw Nation. Most of the U.S. military activity in this region originated in efforts to keep the peace between tribes and to protect the immigrating Southeastern tribes. Fort Towson was rebuilt in the Choctaw Nation; a road from Fort Smith through the Choctaw Nation to the Red River was built–the first road in the new Indian Territory; troops were once again stationed at Fort Smith, and, around the time of this incident, a large stone fortress built there to replace the old stockade.

As this incident shows, whites were already illegally occupying the Indian Territory.

"We moved to Texas from north part of Alabama, and settled high up on the Colorado.[46] My father's name was Goachy. The Pawnees came to our house one morning. Three of my little brothers were at the spring with my child (a girl), there they killed one of my little brothers, and then came to the house. I was in the house and my mother was out—I heard her scream. When I ran out I saw several Indians had hold of her—they struck her down and shot eight arrows into her breast and then shot her with a gun and scalped her.

My father and my oldest brother were out, with a wagon to haul in wood. I saw them killed. They shot at me but missed me. Seeing they had my infant and two little brothers prisoners, I ran to one of them and gave myself up. I done this hoping they might not kill me and that if I should live I might see what became of my babe and little brothers. They stripped me of my clothes and gave me an old worn out blanket to cover my nakedness and to screen my babe from the weather, and made me walk bare footed through the prairies. We were three weeks on the road, and every night my hands were tied behind together. When I came in they made me and my little brothers hold the scalps of my mother and father and two brothers, while they danced around us and mocked at us. We were then divided out—my babe taken from me and I did not see her for two months."

When she was thus telling about her infant she hugged and kissed the little child with a mournful look, often calling it by many lovely epithets. She then renewed her narrative:

"I was put to hard work. They were clearing ground and I had to grub and burn brush. I was abused and whipped every day. Oh, I tell you they are hard masters. But there was nothing that went so hard with me as that of being separated from my child. I knew not where it was, but I know it was not well treated. I can't tell you the half of my sufferings."

I then spoke to her little brother, the eldest one, and asked him how he was treated. His answer was, "bad enough, and the worst of it, I was two months longer among them than the rest."

"What did they give you to eat?"

"Beans and corn, it was all they had, but we did not have enough of that, for sometimes we ate but once in three days, and then did not get enough."

---

[46] This is probably the Canadian River, which was sometimes called the "Rio Colorado."

I asked him how he would like to live among such Indians as we were. He quickly replied, "Very well." He is a smart lively boy. In fact the whole family have the appearance of being well raised, and how fortunate they have been after being cast away as it were by fate to thus be redeemed and have the prospect of now being in the society of their own people again. Relations they have none. The young woman had a languid and melancholy cast, the little boys looked like poor orphans indeed. I did not learn as much about their fate as I wished to. But certainly I never felt more sympathy for any family than this family of prisoners.

From what I have learned from this family I am of the opinion that the Ta we ash or Pawnees as they are sometimes called are the most cruel Indians to prisoners than any tribe with which I am acquainted. It is the custom of all the Indians east of Mississippi to adopt prisoners into their family and to treat them with affection. They—the prisoners and Spaulding—left here today at about 11:00.

We turned out nearly all hands early this morning for a buffalo chase—two fine ones were killed. I saw today for the first time the antelope and also the prairie rabbit the two most fleet animals in this region. The prairie rabbit is very large, about three times as large as the swamp rabbit. The antelope is a beautiful animal at a distance. I know not how they look, but I am in hopes I will kill one before I return, and shall be able to describe it minutely. They are exceedingly wild, but I have had a shot at one today, a large buck, but missed him. The sun was low, and I had to shoot right towards it. Late in the evening I rode to the north part of this prairie and had a glorious view of the bald hills beyond the Washita.

Tim O'Brien

Tim O'Brien is the author of the critically acclalimed war memoir, *If I Die in a Combat Zone*, the novel, *Going After Cacciato*, which won the National Book Award in 1979, and two other novels, *Northern Lights* and *The Nuclear Age*. His most recent work of fiction, *The Things They Carried*, was chosen as one of the ten best books of 1990 by the New York Times Book Review.

Steven Kaplan received his Phd. in Comparative Literature from the University of Tuebingen, Germany and is now an Associate Professor at the University of Southern Colorado. He is working on a full length study of Tim O'Brien's fiction. This interview was conducted in January of 1991 at the Charles Hotel in Cambridge.

An Interview with
Tim O'Brien / *Steven Kaplan*

Kaplan: You've said that you differ from Paul Berlin in *Going After Cacciato* in that he is more of a dreamer than you are. How do you differ from the narrator Tim O'Brien in *The Things They Carried*?

O'Brien: Everything I've written has come partly out of my own concerns as a human being, and often directly out of those concerns, but the story lines themselves, the events of the stories, and the characters in the stories, the places in the stories, are almost all invented, even the Vietnam stuff. If I don't know it I just make it up, trying not to violate the world as I know it. Ninety percent or more of the material in the book is invented, and I invented 90 percent of a new Tim O'Brien, maybe even more than that.

Kaplan: The chapter "On the Rainy River" describes in great detail how close Tim O'Brien came to fleeing to Canada after he received his draft notice. You've depicted this kind of flirtation with draft evasion in almost all of your books. How closely does this particular story reflect your own life?

O'Brien: It's a dramatization of what I felt during the summer of 1968: a kind of moral schizophrenia. Like the Tim O'Brien in the book, I believed the war was wrong and thought that the morally correct thing to do was to flee, to run from it, or else go to jail. But another side of my personality, like the character in the book, felt a kind of gravity pulling me toward the war. The drama of the story, the facts about that character going to the river, meeting somebody, and almost crossing into Canada, were all invented. It was kind of a dramatic enactment of what had been an old, old daydream on my part.

If I were to tell you the truth about the summer of 1968 it would be that I worried a lot. I also played golf and ate hamburgers, but all of that would have been a dramatically empty story. It wouldn't have had the emotional quality of the Rainy River story, where I put a character right on the edge, how I felt psychologically, on the edge.

Kaplan: Many critics said that *The Things They Carried* is a great book, but that it can in no real sense be considered a novel.

O'Brien: Novels have a kind of continuity of plot or of narrative which this book does not have. But it would be unfair for me to say that it's a collection of stories; clearly all of the stories are related and the characters reappear and themes recur, and some of the stories refer back to others, and others refer forwards. I've thought of it as a work of fiction that is neither one nor the other.

Kaplan: Several chapters of *Going After Cacciato*, like much of *The Things They Carried*, were initially published as short stories. Did you think of *Cacciato* as a novel while you were working on it?

O'Brien: Almost from the moment of conception. It's a matter of feel. It's also a matter of how you're going to work with the materials.

Kaplan: In all of your previous books there is at least one strongly delineated character, someone who sticks in the reader's mind for a long time, such as Cacciato, or William Cowling. I don't know, however, if I would say the same thing about *The Things They Carried*. Has your focus somehow turned away from character?

O'Brien: No, not really. To me there is a dominant character in *The Things They Carried* in the Tim O'Brien character, but he's

"I think that way too much has been made of gender by both sides. . . . we're not that different"

rendered more as a teller of the story, I guess in the same way Marlow is used by Conrad. I can't picture much about Marlow. He's a voice and a commentator. He analyzes, and at times he behaves in his own stories. He explains, for example, at the end of *Heart of Darkness* what he did when he returned to London— that he visited the fiancé and told her what had happened. He's not a judging figure, but a consciousness, both telling the story and vaguely participating in it.

Kaplan: Is that how you use O'Brien?

O'Brien: Yes, although the O'Brien character is much more a participant. He gets shot, and he plans revenge. He does a lot of things in the story, both in the present and in the past.

Kaplan: Were you more interested in the issues of storytelling than in the storyteller?

O'Brien: In part. I can see that young girl in her shorts. I can see little Linda. And I can see Mitchell Sanders and his yo-yo. I can see these things. But because it is interrelated fictions and not a novel, one can't have beyond that O'Brien consciousness a dominant figure who is going to stay with you through it all. Rat will tell a story, and then Mitchell Sanders will tell another. The girl dancing will be another. This kind of form precludes a typical, dominant character.

Kaplan: In both *The Nuclear Age* and *The Things They Carried* a female character undergoes a transformation from a kind of cheerleader/hometown sweetheart to a terrorist/guerilla warrior. Are you somehow trying to comment through your female characters

"Good stories have to do with an awakening where someone is jolted out of complacency to confront a new self."

---

on the nature of the man's world in which your novels take place?

O'Brien: I am. The materials in the stories are what they are. I'm a man, and I write about things. I often write about war, and war in our culture has been historically a man's milieu. Yet it seems to me that it is unfair to half of the population to unnecessarily exclude female participation in male events. It would be more fun, it would be more instructive, it would be more artistic, more beautiful, to include as much as possible the whole of humanity in these stories. Also, it's interesting to test in one's imagination, almost as one would test a hypothesis, the actions and reactions of a female heart to situations to which they are not accustomed.

Kaplan: Do you think there are differences between the way men and women react to situations of extreme stress?

O'Brien: I don't. I think that too much has been made of gender, way too much has been made of it, by both sides. Under situations of stress and in situations of incredible danger and trauma, women are capable, as men are, of great evil, of great good, and of all shades in between.

What I am trying to show, what I am trying to open the door to, is the possibility that we aren't that different. We're different, yes, but we're not *that* different. We all experience anger. We experience lust. We experience terror. We experience curiosity and fascination for that which repels us. All of us.

Kaplan: Many of your female characters seem to be exaggerated embodiments of stereotypical characteristics, such as innocence—the cheerleader—and tenderness—the hometown sweetheart. Aren't you somehow saying that they are in fact different from men?

O'Brien: No. I do the same thing when I portray men. My chief male characters have been almost prototypes of innocence. I think of Paul Berlin, a midwestern kid, and I think of Tim O'Brien in *The Things They Carried*. I also think of my Montana guy in *The Nuclear Age*, William Cowlings.

All of my characters are shaken out of a state of stasis—a kind of innocence, a kind of belief in the world that's grounded in a thoughtless traditionalism, and by thoughtless I mean that it is accepted or taken for granted—by some kind of outside, global event. In all of the books except maybe *Northern Lights* some outside event intrudes on that innocence. The characters, like Rip Van Winkle, are shaken awake and forced to confront their own naivete, their own jejune acceptance of an order.

Kaplan: Critics have frequently compared you to Hemingway, but what you just said sounds a lot more like Fitzgerald.

O'Brien: I also have a lot in common with Conrad in many ways, especially when I think of *Lord Jim*. Good stories somehow have to do with an awakening into a new world, something new and true, where someone is jolted out of a kind of complacency and forced to confront a new set of circumstances or a new self. You know, the father dies, or a ship is wrecked like in *Robinson Crusoe*, or a new order has to be established, or an effort to establish a new order has to be made. Fiction, storytelling, has to do with those kinds of crucial changes in a character's life.

Kaplan: That might be true of characters in conventional fiction, but I don't know to what extent that formula could be used to describe some of your more absurd characters, such as Ebeneezer Keezer and Nethro in *The Nuclear Age*, who don't seem to develop at all. When you created these two characters did you consciously distort their personalities?

O'Brien: Sure. *The Nuclear Age* in general was meant to be a big cartoon of the nuclear age, with everything heightened and exaggerated. William Cowling's own fears are way beyond the ordinary quiet terror that most of us have lived with over the last fifty years. Sarah, as a character, is blown way out of proportion. Events in the story are blown way out of proportion, the way Trudeau does it in *Doonesbury*. It's got kind of a Popeye feel. You know, the muscles are bigger.

Kaplan: You did a parody of Hemingway's first novel, *The Sun Also Rises*, in your own first novel, *Northern Lights*. Could you talk a little bit about the similarities and differences between these two books.

O'Brien: I tried to make fun of Hemingway. I respect Hemingway's work, and some of it I love. But sometimes I find myself being irritated by a kind of macho simplicity and by the way women are treated almost as little pawns to be moved around from place to place. That's not always true of his women, but often it is true, I think. There are approximately forty pages in *Northern Lights* where I parody Hemingway, though I probably would not have done so if I had known at the time that good fiction is not ordinarily the place for parody. I wish now I hadn't done it, though I must admit that it was really fun. I don't think I've ever enjoyed writing so much as I enjoyed the month or so I spent on those forty pages.

Kaplan: Like Hemingway, you seem to be preoccupied with the

"One tries to wrestle new meanings and new stories out of the concerns of one's life."

question of courage. Many of the incidents in *If I Die* appear in a new form in *The Things They Carried*, as do themes of desertion and courage.

O'Brien: Some of the events are the same in the roughest, narrative kinds of ways. I don't know what else to say. I guess I go back to material in the way that every writer goes back to his or her concerns for the world. My concerns as a human being and my concerns as an artist have at some point intersected in Vietnam— not just in the physical place, but in the spiritual and moral terrain of Vietnam. They intersected there in the way that the Midwest-Princeton linear flow of Fitzgerald's life intersected with the aftermath of World War I. There was an intersection of values, of what was and what was to come, that I'll always go back to, and I'd be crazy not to.

Conrad kept returning over and over again to the same venue, which was the sea, and the microcosm aboard a ship frames his work. Shakespeare kept writing about kings, to eternity. But one tries to wrestle new meanings and new stories out of the concerns of one's life. One has to care about the material. I care about issues of courage, and I care about issues of storytelling, and I care about issues of mysteriousness, and I care about cyclical patterns of plot. In *The Things They Carried* the events of the war are kind of recycled over and over again, and so are my characters' histories and thoughts. I try to make those things I care about as a person interesting.

Kaplan: Unlike most of the other writers and filmmakers who have dealt with the war, you devote very little space in your books to war crimes. Why is that?

"What fascinates us about character, about other human beings, is that we just will never be that person."

O'Brien: Most war crimes, in my experience, are little episodes of war, little fragments of war. Something such as shooting one innocent human being for fun, let's say a farmer in a rice paddy, is to me in its magnitude of evil as bad as, say, fire bombing Tokyo. Quantity is not a measure of evil, in my opinion. The shooting of the water buffalo in *The Things They Carried* is an act of evil. It's a little thing, the death of a water buffalo. And yet my hope as a writer is that those accruing acts of evil will touch a reader's heart more than a grandiose description of the fire bombing of a village, or the napalming of a village, where you don't see the corpses, you don't know the corpses, you don't witness the death in any detail. It's somehow made abstract, bloodless.

Because it is such a horrible and huge event, war in general is seen abstractly by most of us. Even the declarations about war, such as war is hell, war is evil and so on, are bloodless and abstract because they're so broad. The only way that the horror of war can mean anything to us is through small detailed vignettes or episodes of evil. Finally, I guess I should also say that as a human being I have never witnessed any large-scale atrocities. I think that by and large, large-scale atrocities are a rare phenomenon of war, unless one includes things like the bombings of cities, which are, at least in my way of thinking, atrocities. But I have never seen My Lais. I have never seen concentration camps. I have never seen any large-scale murder. I've seen the trappings of it, and I've seen the surface of it, but I've never seen anyone die in those kinds of situations. As a writer you almost have to trust in that, not which you have necessarily witnessed, but to which you feel some kind of proximity, and I've never felt that kind of proximity to large-scale, blatant atrocities.

Kaplan: How do you react to scenes like the one in *Apocalypse*

Now where a village is attacked and destroyed so Colonel Kilgore can hold a surfing contest?

O'Brien: I could almost imagine that thing being staged, with people shouting through megaphones. It looked artificial, although parts of *Apocalypse Now* looked absolutely wonderful. That scene in particular, however, struck me as gimmicky. It didn't seem very horrible to me either. It seemed a little bit like World War II movies where there was no sense of real gut-wrenching savagery and horror, much of which the rest of the movie does have. The end of the movie seems to be much more horrible, the killing of that calf, the butchering of it.

Kaplan: One of the problems with films like *Apocalypse Now* is that they tend to emphasize the craziness of the war without coming to terms with the suffering of the Vietnamese people. Do you feel you have dealt with the Vietnamese people as closely as you would have liked to?

O'Brien: More closely than I would have liked to. I didn't know them. They didn't know me. One can't pretend to know what one doesn't. One can use one's imagination and try to identify with villagers and with particular human beings, soldiers who are Vietnamese. But to do it successfully you have to somehow be grounded in that which would somehow fuel their imaginations. One can't simply impose a Western imagination on those people and come up with anything meaningful. If I were capable of imagining the Vietnamese I would do it. But I'm not.

Kaplan: A speaker at a conference on the literature of the Vietnam War called the Vietnamese people the great lost factor of the

Vietnam War, and he said it was the obligation of American writers to deal with them. Do you agree?

O'Brien: No! The natural responsibility for telling the Vietnamese side of the story should and does rest with the Vietnamese themselves, with the Vietnamese writers. At a conference here in Boston last summer this very issue was discussed with three Vietnamese. All of us, all of the American writers, said to various degrees and in various ways that we've been criticized for not giving the Vietnamese point of view and the Vietnamese writers just laughed and said, that's *our* job. I think, by and large, in American fiction the Vietnamese people have ended up as stereotyped cartoon figures or as puppets.

Kaplan: What are some of the other ideas and issues that concern you?

O'Brien: My answer to that has to do with the book I am working on now. Do you remember the story about Judge Crater, the guy who in the 1930s in New York City went out of his house and just disappeared? That's an earthly representation of a larger mystery. What happens when we die? Where do we go? We'll never know. In this world we'll never know.

What we don't know is inherently intriguing to the human spirit. That includes big metaphysical things like death and God, and it includes little discrete daily things like, what is she thinking now as I'm having this drink at this bar? There is always that mystery because one can't read other people's minds. What fascinates us in part about character, about other human beings, is that we just will never be that person, live that person's life.

The mystery of what we can't know is what's dominating the

"In the stories I'm trying to write, the ultimate mystery of the mystery story has to do with the unknowable."

novel I'm working on right now. It's structured in a sense as a mystery, I suppose. A man wakes up and his wife is gone, no fights, no notes, no explanation at all. She's just physically, forever gone, with no reason. The book is a series of hypotheses about what might have become of her. He imagines her saying, "I got on a train and went to Seattle. I drowned." So it's the man trying to enter his wife's imagination, looking for explanations.

Kaplan: There are several elements in both *Cacciato* and in *The Nuclear Age* that are strongly reminiscent of detective fiction. Do you see similarities between what you have done in your writings and what some of the masters of crime fiction, like Poe and Borges, have done in theirs?

O'Brien: Not really, no. I don't read much detective fiction. I've read some, now and then. To me great crime fiction would be stuff like *The Brothers Karamazov, Crime and Punishment, Les Mis´erables,* or a great short story by John Fowles called "Poor Cocoa." Ordinary detective fiction as I know it is kind of inconsequential in its concern for the surface: for "who did it?" and "how was it done?" Those are the kind of practical, mechanical questions, which are interesting, but ultimately forgettable. Once you know who did it, you don't care who did it, because you know. But in the story I'm trying to write, and in the stories I've told, the ultimate mystery of the mystery story has to do with the unknowable.

Kaplan: What you just described could also be applied to Conrad's method in *Heart of Darkness* and *Lord Jim.* The narrator is a kind of detective looking for answers to things that cannot be answered, for answers to the unknowable.

"Fiction relies on a reader's participation in the development of character."

O'Brien: Exactly. Those are good examples. He's asking himself in *Heart of Darkness* about Kurtz as he tells the story. There are all kinds of statements such as, "This may have happened," and there's no opportunity to really know the facts about Kurtz, because by the time Marlow reaches him, Kurtz has become unknowable. All he can do is mutter "the horror." He doesn't say much else.

Kaplan: You talk a great deal in *The Things They Carried* about storytelling. What psychological and social functions do you think storytelling has?

O'Brien: That's a tough one, a big one. There are all kinds of answers, but the answers that matter to me, personally, are those I talk about in the book itself. Good stories can be true or untrue. It doesn't really matter too much, provided that the story does to the spirit what stories should do, which is to entertain, but entertain in the highest way, entertain your brain and your stomach, and your heart, and your erotic zones, and make you laugh.

Kaplan: Ebeneezer and Nethro are definitely among your funniest characters. They remind me of the characters in Harold Pinter's plays. Have you ever written a play?

O'Brien: I wrote a radio play for public radio called *Your Play* about ten years ago based on a chapter from *Cacciato*.

Kaplan: Do you think your novels or your characters would come across well on the screen?

O'Brien: Fiction relies more on a reader's participation in the development of character. You're not presented with concrete embodiments of a character's face. Film seems to be a little bit more passive as a medium.

I guess what I am trying to say is that I've felt a bit disappointed in seeing, say, Huck Finn's face in a film after having made up my own. To that extent I'm not sure I want any of my books made into movies. I'm certainly willing to take the money that they've been paying me for years, and I'll keep taking it, while still hoping that they'll never make one. That's the ideal world.

Kaplan: You have said that the purpose of writing fiction is to explore moral quandaries, that the best fiction has a character who is confronted with having to make a difficult choice. How does this apply to Tim O'Brien in *The Things They Carried*. Outside of the Rainy River segment, how does it apply to the book as a whole?

O'Brien: Well, there is the Rainy River section, and one can't deny it. It explains so much, and it also determines so much of why the O'Brien character behaves as he does in the book. But in the course of the book, the O'Brien character makes all kinds of choices. There's the "Ghost Soldiers" chapter, with the decision to get revenge. And there is Kiowa's death, all kinds of choices are made there—choosing to live and let Kiowa die. There is also the choice of what one does to come to terms with a whole history.

I can't think of a story that isn't structured around choices, except maybe for a couple of Flannery O'Connor stories. I'm thinking of "A Good Man Is Hard to Find," which is difficult to talk about in this way. I mean, who chooses what? Something just happens to those poor people. They go out and they're massacred. Yet what makes the story come alive are the things that those characters choose to say and do in the course of this horrible, inexplicable

*"One's attention is on trying to put
down one word after another with a kind of
grace and beauty."*

---

thing. They didn't choose for this to happen to them, but they do choose how to behave as it happens to them.

The reason choice seems to me important as a word and as a way for me to think about stories is that it involves values. It's most interesting when the choices involve things of equally compelling value, when you say, God, I really want that, but I also want that. Or I really don't want that, and I don't want that either.

Kaplan: When I first proposed writing a book on you, you said that it might be premature since you are still in the middle of your career. Where do you hope to be in the next five to ten years?

O'Brien: I don't know. That's another tough one to answer. You learn something every day, and what you learn is particulars, little tiny things that have to do with sentences. Is that a rotten sentence, and why is it a rotten sentence? It could be rotten for billions of reasons, and you learn new reasons every day. Sometimes when you first write a sentence you don't realize there is something wrong with it, and it might be a week or it could be a second before you realize, oh that's the reason why it's not a good sentence. It's the particular things that are sparked in my mind, and if there were one important thing I could say in the whole interview it would be that my attention is more on this stuff that we're talking about right now than it is on grand things. The grand things float. They're around you all the time, and if you try to pay too much attention to them you kill the mentality of the writing itself. And so you kill the grand idea. One's attention as a writer is on trying to put down one word after another with a kind of grace and a kind of beauty that's a constant, never-ending balancing act of billions of variables.

KNOCK, KNOCK, LEAVE ME ALONE
/ Paul S. Brownfield

"THERE WAS A TIME in my life when I was addicted to non-profit organizations," Evie confessed, gazing at her audience. There were plates of nachos at some of the tables, people digging in. It made her feel like the exhibitionist in the family, or TV, something you watched while you ate. "I canvassed for everybody—Amnesty International, Greenpeace, Earth First, Pluto Second. I can tell you about my problem now, but that's only because I'm better. I can say, 'Hello, my name is Evelyn Singer and I...I...I want you to sign my petition.' I'm not fully recovered, I still collect signatures. Not for any specific cause, I just collect them. I still protest against things, but little things. Like the other day, I saw my boyfriend Ray throwing out half a banana and I screamed, 'Save The Fruit! Save the Fruit!' "

" 'Save the Fruit!' " Evie said into the mike one more time; it came out as a high-pitched squeal. She still had a tendency to repeat her punchlines, just to make sure. She used to think they were laughing at a heckler loose out there, who was making funny rebuttals in some special heckler's language that only audiences understood. She used to spot her imaginary roommates, career-minded Nancy and macrobiotic Phil, sitting at a table smack in the middle of the club and glaring back, insulted that she was using them in her act. She used to doubt her jokes and so she read a manual. "If three audiences in a row don't laugh," it said, "throw the material out." She'd had a lot of three-audiences-in-a-row at first. But now, no more hallucinations about hecklers speaking in coded tongues. She had this regular Thursday night spot at Ziggy's, in the Financial District, playing to San Francisco's jaded urban professionals. They liked her; she was jaded, too—though, she assured herself, only for career purposes. In three weeks, she would be on a cable special.

"I met my boyfriend Ray in a class that guaranteed we'd be fluent in Swahili in six weeks. I had a dream about going to Africa and feeding people. Ray, he was just fed up with the English language, said he was shopping around for fairer grammar rules. Now when we make love he moans in Swahili, conjugating verbs."

Evie looked out at the audience, spotted a couple. She could always tell a first date by the way the man and the woman looked at each other after every punchline to see which one was laughing. Evie was their common denominator. If they both liked her act there would be a second date. And then a third and then a fourth, when the sex would be "good enough"—like a rough draft—and then they would be married. Evie knew she wouldn't be invited to the wedding but she did expect a card, something with vines and flowers on it that said: "Thanks for bringing us together. Love, Harry and Jill."

It went something like that, anyway, what she did for a living.

After her show, Evie went to dinner with her boyfriend Terence, a graphic artist. They'd been seeing each other for two years and had already talked about which organs they'd give each other in a medical emergency. They were in love.

They were.

Tonight they went to a Thai place that had just opened south of Market, and after an hour of waiting the food arrived—tiny food.

"It looks like an aerial view of Chinese hieroglyphics," Evie said.

"Can I ask you something, Evie?"

He would ask her to marry him. He would tell her to move out of her apartment, move in with him, get married and have kids. He would tell her that he wanted to spend the rest of his life with her, that he loved her. Either that, or he'd ask where the bathroom was. That was what Evie loved about their relationship— the *suspense*.

"You know," Terence said, "I can't remember the last time I had a serious discussion with you. And then tonight, I was watching you onstage and I thought, 'she's more serious about Ray than she is about me.'"

"You're jealous of my imaginary boyfriend?" Evie said. She removed the straw from her tonic water, leaned forward, and poked him on the chin. "That's sweet."

The waitress appeared, to check up on things. She looked like Madonna, Evie thought, except she had black hair and none of the snappy crucifix jewelry. "How's everything?" she asked.

"Does mine come with a microscope?" Evie said.

The waitress grinned. "It's nouvelle Thai, what can I tell you."

"Looks more like nouvelle Lilliputian to me. What do you think, Terence?"

"It's definitely small," he told them.

"This is good," Evie told the waitress, holding up a sliver of chicken. "I'm trying to keep my intake down to 500 molecules a day."

"Can I get you anything else?"

"Another glass of wine," Terence said.

"And a Nutri-System shake for me." The waitress left, and Evie tipped her plate. "What you think? Drip art. I call it, 'My Order.' Anyway, so what were you saying?"

"It can wait," Terence said.

It waited until they were in his car. Terence was dropping her off at her apartment, not taking her into his. "There was a time, I know, when I encouraged you to do stand-up," he said. "But something's happened. It's like you're cheating on me. Sometimes I think I should give you an ultimatum, your punchlines, or me."

"Can't we work out a schedule?"

"You see? It's become impossible to be serious with you."

"No it hasn't," Evie said. She straightened herself in the passenger seat. She was petite, and had a tendency to be swallowed up by safety belts. "Here, I'll show you. Tell me something serious."

"I'm not happy in the relationship."

"OK, now tell me something more serious."

"I can't see you anymore."

"You can't?," Evie said, "Shit, 29 years old, and I'm already shrinking!"

"Good night, Evie."

"Wait," she heard herself say. She rummaged around in her mind, her cluttered attic of a mind, full of old jokes. Somewhere, stuffed beneath the material about her roommates and the routine about her father, there was a serious thought, a genuine feeling. But she couldn't find it now, she needed a whole day, Van Morrison's *Astral Weeks* playing in the background. She needed to change into sweats, haul out serious appliances.

"I really like Van Morrison," Evie said.

Terence sighed. "I know, Evie."

"I think *Astral Weeks* is a very sad album."

Terence unlocked the emergency brake. "There are tons of people who think *Astral Weeks* is a sad album, Evie. I need something better. I need sentences that start with 'I'm excited about this' or 'I'm unhappy about that.'" Terence ran his hand over his receding blond hair. Evie's hair was frizzy and dark, uncooperative. She just let it grow and grow, and then when she feared it would attack in her sleep, she had it tamed. "Do you remember how we met?" Terence asked.

"At an extension class."

"The photography class, right. You did some self-portraits. Very expressive. Go back and look at them. Especially the one where you're brushing your hair in the mirror. That's the woman I was interested in."

She didn't have the heart to tell Terence she'd defaced that picture. She'd cut out her head and replaced it with Carmen Miranda's. Suddenly she saw the vast distance between her and Terence. She liked produce on her head, Terence only used a little styling gel. It didn't seem fair that their relationship should hinge on her desire to wear fruit, but there it was. She leaned over and kissed Terence hard on the lips. "I need you," she murmured, pushed open the car door and ran up her front steps, because whenever she expressed a true emotion she got this urge to run, run run run.

She found her imaginary roommates, Nancy and Phil, in the bathroom. They didn't go to see her perform anymore, but they were always around when she was home. Evie had given them all sorts of pretensions, and she noshed on them, as if they were leftover Chinese food. Nancy ran her own casting agency for TV commercial spots. There were piles of her mail on the table next to the front door, mostly postcard-size publicity stills, of pretty women, and men who looked like Phil, only waxier. Phil was a 30-ish attorney who posted his meditation schedule under a banana magnet on the refrigerator. He wore clothes from vintage stores by way of the dry cleaners. Evie was pretty sure his glasses were fake but she also thought it would cause serious roommate friction if she asked to try them on.

"I'm going to be on a cable special," Evie told them, looking in the mirror for moustache hairs. "For up-and-coming comics."

"Sellout," Nancy said.

"Tool," Phil said.

Nancy handed him the hammer. He nailed a hot water bottle to the bathroom wall.

"What are you doing?" Evie asked.

"I'm making a medicinal collage," Phil said. So far he had hung a stethoscope, a thermometer on a string, the water bottle, and an editorial from the Chronicle about chicken soup. Nancy was sitting on top of the toilet, her feet on the seat cover, overseeing.

"Cable television," Phil said, positing with the hammer, "is a frightening concept."

"But we have cable," Evie said.

Paul S. Brownfield

"As a casting agent," Nancy said, "I need to see what in L.A. they consider a public access look."

They worked as a team against her, Nancy and Phil, played off of her insecurities. They said things to her like, "You have to open up to people, Evie. Feelings are a 365 day commitment." Whenever they sensed she was ready to move out on them, to chuck her comedy career and work 9 to 5, have 9 to 5 emotions, they shrouded her in perky warmth. "We really love you," they said, putting their arms around her. "Really, we think you're funny. Really we do."

Phil produced another nail from his pocket. Nancy handed him an enema bag.

"You're going to hang an enema bag?" Evie said.

"Lighten up," Phil said.

Later that night Evie called Terence, to ask if he'd broken up with her in the car. After five rings he answered, his voice croaky from sleep. "Hello?" he said. "Hello? Who's that?"

She didn't know what to do, so she breathed heavily, three deep pants, and hung up. Phil and Nancy had gone to sleep, and she didn't feel like waking them. It was just her then, sitting up in the Murphy bed at three in the morning, feeling the crevices in her knees.

The next day Evie went to her three-day-a-week volunteer job, answering phones for a panic disorder hotline. People called to talk about anxiety attacks, the pain of them, and Evie told jokes on herself, until she imagined that the caller's panic episode had been reduced to a minor irritant, something along the lines of a mosquito bite.

"My doctor thinks I should start taking medication," a caller once told her.

"I don't think I can recommend drugs," Evie had said. "I took an anti-depressant once and when I woke up the next morning, I'd glitter-dusted my entire body."

This was one of the reasons she loved doing jokes: you could take a serious thing, flip it over and see it again, see it funny, like a magical two-headed coin.

"And then at some point during my senior year, I just got bloated, fed up." Sometimes Evie couldn't help lapsing into parts of her routine. "Greenpeace, Earth First, Al Anon, a cooperative gardening class—I was so full of meetings, of self-actualization and fringe causes, that I expected to start vomiting Amnesty International gift items. I lost weight. I feared the mailman. The poor mailman! I was on every non-profit organization's hit list. I began to feel more and more like one of those mailing labels. I wondered how many interns had licked the back of my name, stuck me on an envelope. I felt cheap, licked all over, by the whole non-profit world. I didn't want to make any more friends in controlled settings."

"Did you mention a cooperative gardening class during that speech?" asked the caller, an elderly woman.

"Yes," Evie said.

"Could I have their number, dear?"

If, when Evie answered her phone, the person said he had a gun to his head right then, or was holding a fistful of sleeping pills, she immediately transferred the call; Evie didn't know how to seriously talk anyone out of anything.

In the office she sat next to Gerald, a man in his fifties who'd been a radio psychiatrist in New York City until his ratings dipped. Now he was in San Francisco, counseling couples on the brink of divorce, talking others out of anxiety attacks. It made her slightly nervous to sit next to him—someone who dealt so often with people on the edge of things would surely find her cliff, too. When he wasn't answering his phone Gerald listened to a local psychiatrist's radio call-in show. It was all about love problems. Gerald talked back to the radio, said, "No-no-no-no" when he thought the psychiatrist was giving bad advice, which was often.

She was on the phone late that afternoon when a familiar voice came out of Gerald's radio. "I've tried to tell her," the caller was saying. "I really have. Three, four times. But she keeps joking it away." It was Terence's voice. "Last night I actually said it. I told her I couldn't see her anymore."

"And what did she say?" the psychiatrist asked.

"She said, 'Oh, no, don't tell me I'm already shrinking.'" The psychiatrist chuckled, but Terence didn't, and neither did Evie. Wait, she remembered suddenly, I have a panicked person on the phone with me.

"Hello?" Evie said.

"I'm still here," the man said.

"Listen, I'm going to transfer you."

"Wait, you mentioned a cooperative gardening class. Do you know how I'd get in touch with them?"

Paul S. Brownfield

Evie transferred the call, reached over and turned up the volume on Gerald's radio.

"Well," the psychiatrist said, "it sounds to me like you're dealing with a person who uses her sense of humor as a defense mechanism, as a way of avoiding complex emotions."

"I know," Terence said. "So what do I do?"

"What do you want to do?"

"It's tough," Terence said. "I feel both loved and humiliated by her."

"But remember," the psychiatrist said. "The reason she tells jokes is because she's not strong enough to be a serious person. You shouldn't feel humiliated. She should."

"No-no-no-no," Gerald said. Evie looked at him. By now she was feeling nauseous, slightly terrified. She wanted to grab the radio, turn it off.

"I can't tell her how I feel in person," Terence was saying. "I can't tell her over the phone, because then she just comes back with a joke. That's partly why I called. I know she sits next to someone at work who listens to your show."

Gerald looked immediately at Evie.

"OK," the doctor said. "What do you want to tell her?"

Terence sighed, a big sigh that came out over the radio. "Well, the thing is, I met someone else. I didn't mean to, but this new person helped me deal with how nervous and inadequate Ev— my girlfriend made me feel. I finally felt I had someone I could confide in, someone I could be serious about."

"Are you OK, Evie?" Gerald asked. "You look pale."

"No-no-no-no-no," Evie said.

"Is that another joke?" Gerald said, softly, his voice hinting at expensive sessions.

"I can't tell you how refreshing my new relationship feels," Terence said. "To be with someone who doesn't turn me into material."

It was like a *Twilight Zone*. One day a comic wakes up to discover the world has lost its sense of humor. Without jokes, what will she do? Evie felt violated, as if someone had broken into her heart, ransacked the place and taken her jokes hostage. The ransom note said only: "Get real." More than anything she wanted to be onstage right now, making people laugh, setting her world right again. She looked at Gerald, who had his arms folded, waiting for her response, patient as a therapist. There were phone lines lit up but he wasn't answering them. Evie glared at him. "Knock, knock," she said.

"Who's—"

"Leave me alone."

"My boyfriend Ray just broke up with me," Evie told her audience the following week. "Actually he didn't dump me in person, he called one of those radio sex psychologists. I'm at home and I get this phone call from my friend Brenda. 'Evie,' she says, 'turn on the radio, your boyfriend is breaking up with you!'"

She had labored hard for this punchline, and when the audience laughed at it she felt like taking them all out to dinner. "The sex doctor said that I'm a person who uses her sense of humor as a way of avoiding complex emotions," she told them. "That I'm not strong enough to be a serious person, so I joke. And joke and joke and joke."

"Anyway," she went on, gripping the mike stand. "My father is a high school math teacher. He's been doing this for 29 years, and by now, he's just totally oblivious. Not too long ago I went to his class, and there was this kid who kept passing me notes. He was kind of spooky looking, you know—crew cut, key ring through his nose, plaid hunting shirt, panty hose on his head—we're talking illegitimate Son of Sam. And he's passing me these notes like, 'I have my mother's gas card and I'm angry.' I finally had to write back, so I put, 'How about if we all sneeze at three o'clock. Pass it on.'"

Sydney Frank, the producer of the cable special, brought Evie to his table after the show. He was an older man, with silver hair. Beneath his dark blazer he was wearing a t-shirt that said, "Bo Knows Your Wife."

"Just super, super-fine," he said. "The bit about the roommates, the medicinal collage, wonderful stuff."

"Thanks."

"A couple things, though. At one point, you were doing a bit about your boyfriend and the sex doctor. Which was clever, don't get me wrong. But you weren't doing it like you should. You weren't doing it like comedy."

"How was I doing it?" Evie asked.

"Well, I can only tell you it came off as a downer. The good comedians, what they do is they take all the crappage in their life and they turn it into laughs. Into an upper. Not a downer, an upper." He was thrusting both thumbs towards the ceiling.

"Mmmm," Evie said. "Exactly." She had read in her comedian's manual that you weren't supposed to disagree with producers.

"And don't give us theories about why you joke. That spoils the party. We don't want to hear theories." Sydney Frank was shaking his head, and Evie saw his hair slide ever so slightly to the left. "When people come to a club, they check their suffering at the door. They wanna hear how much you suffer, OK? The trick is to make it funny. You get my meaning?"

"Mmmm. Make my suffering funny."

"Look," he said, removing dental floss from his jacket pocket. "You haven't come into your own yet. You haven't made the leap." His right hand soared across the table. Then he started flossing. "You're what I'd call a middle class comic," he said. "You're getting dates in a major city but it's not like you're doing the Hollywood Squares. No one's saying, 'Evie Singer to block.' But you're a damn funny lady, OK? I'm serious, damn funny."

When Evie came home from the club that night she found Phil in the kitchen. He liked to cook, but more than that he liked to delight his friends. He made politically correct birthday cakes for his friends, jellos that spelled, "Peace Now." He was never specific about which peace. Tonight he was making brie whiz. Friends were coming over on Sunday. The 49ers were on TV.

"Brie whiz?" Evie asked, her Finn Crisp still poised. She was his taster.

"I just want to make sure nothing toxic will happen," Phil said.

"Looks all right."

"This is what you make for trashy postmodern people," Phil said.

"Then shouldn't you be tasting it?"

"Save it for the act, Evie."

She felt her stomach drop right then, as if Phil had said, "You smell like cigarettes."

On Saturday, Evie went to see *The Diary of Anne Frank* at the Red Vic. Every time they played the movie she went. They had dorm couches instead of seats in the theater. She sank down, and while Anne hid from the Nazis and wondered about puberty, Evie picked at the foam padding where the upholstery had come off. She liked the feeling of being Anne, a teenage Jew trapped by identity and circumstance, who escaped to a diary, a private life. By the end of the movie she had a wad of foam that was tennis ball size, and she threw it at the screen as the credits rolled.

Later, walking back to her car, through the Haight, past the sweet-smelling ice cream shops and the homeless who neutralized the smell, Evie thought about quitting this life of punchlines. She wondered if there was a self-help group for the compulsively jokey. Maybe she could start her own. They could do implosion therapy, like one of the smoke-out centers. Sit in a circle, in Nixon masks, telling each other "Knock, Knock" jokes until they all just started weeping. "It all started when I was 10," Evie would tell them. "My mother wanted to have a veal for Thanksgiving and I said, 'Mom, my God, what would the Indians think?'"

That afternoon Evie decided to drive across the Bay and tell her parents she was going to be on a cable special. She could never go to see her parents unless she had news; likewise, whenever Evie's mother called, she had to begin with, "Something odd, Evelyn..."

"Something odd," her mother would say, "I found an old sweater of yours in my closet the other day."

"You did?" Evie would say, but neither of them had any idea what they were talking about.

Her parents still lived in El Cerrito, in a one-story house with a front lawn that to Evie had always looked like the stubble of a dying man.

"Hi, Mom," Evie said, standing on the other side of the screen door.

"Something odd," her mother said, fooling with the lock. "This door has been acting up ever since that winter we had. It must still be swollen from all that rain. Your father's at the supermarket." She opened the door and gave Evie her cheek. Evie kissed it.

"I'm going to be on cable," Evie said.

"Cable, huh?" her mother said, stepping away and looking her daughter up and down, as if Evie had lost weight. "Your father and I'll have to watch. When is it?"

"They're taping next Saturday. But the show won't be on TV for a couple of weeks."

"Well, come on in, then."

Evie followed her mother to the kitchen. In the living room the television was on, tuned to the Home Shopping Network. Whenever Evie came home she made a point not to look around too much. She didn't go into her old bedroom. She worried she would discover some former version of herself, a little girl in a pink dress and pigtails, sprawled over a huge piece of construction paper drawing ugly black suns.

"Now don't get excited," her mother said, when they'd sat down in the kitchen with a pitcher of iced tea. Her mother was in a

Paul S. Brownfield

robe, and she put her hand over her breast, as if she were about to recite the Pledge of Allegiance. "I have a cyst."

"You do?"

"Don't worry, it's nothing serious. But tell me about you. How's your job?"

"I'm a comic, Mom. I don't have a job."

"You always were a funny person."

"It's what I do for a living," Evie said. Her parents had never seen her perform. They still wanted her to be a nurse, or a teacher, or a lawyer. They thought stand-up comics stood in subway stations, telling jokes for loose change. Evie had only done this once. "Is the cyst serious?" she asked.

"Nothing serious. So you're not going to have a career?"

"I have a career."

"Right," her mother said. "The funny business," and they sat there, nodding at each other.

Sydney Frank called on Thursday, two days before the taping, to talk about what Evie should wear.

"We didn't get a chance to discuss this the other night," he said. "About your persona."

"Uhm," Evie said.

"Here's how I see you." Evie heard little squeaks over the phone, Sydney Frank flossing. "I see you in black, to show us you're on the edge of darkness, but with a bright ribbon or some kind of deal in your hair. You're a brunette, so you can zest it up a bit. You know who you remind me of? The character in that book, *Sheila Levine Is Dead and Living in New York*. You know that book?

"She tried to kill herself," Evie protested.

"Yeah. Funny stuff. Think Sheila."

That night Evie woke from a dream in which she came home on a Saturday after seeing *The Diary of Anne Frank* and caught Phil and Nancy in the bathroom, wearing Nixon masks, slaughtering the fatted calf for Thanksgiving. She watched them, hacking at the carcass, blood all over their arms, their clothes. "As a casting agent," Nancy said, "I need to know what in L.A. they consider a Biblical look." "And I just got home," Phil said, his fake glasses bloodied.

She got out of bed and went into the bathroom, stared at Phil's medicinal collage. Since the enema bag, he had added band-aids, Q-tips, and a Pepto Bismol label. She searched the medicine cabinet, found a tube of zinc ointment, turned towards the collage. She got up on a chair, so she could reach over it all. "Bathroom Humor," she wrote, with zinc ointment, and sat on the floor, cowering, because it appeared she had no will power.

"I just called to see how you were doing," Evie said to Terence. It was five in the morning. She had decided to call Terence, then go for a walk through the Mission, staring at fruit shrapnel from the grocer's sidewalk stands, thinking about this phone call to Terence. Contemplative, early morning walks would be part of her new regime.

"I guess you heard the radio show," Terence said.

"Tell me something serious," Evie said. Her voice was soft, on the edge of tears.

"Ah, Evie, not this again. I can't be your straight man at five in the morning."

"Can't you tell me something serious?"

"What do you want me to say?"

"I don't know. But I want to try to hear it. Let's meet. Right now. I want to make love with you right now, this instant. Through the phone. I want us both to close our eyes and feel each other." Evie heard his toilet flush. "You're with someone?" she said.

"Yes, Evie, yes I am. What'd you think?"

"True story," the woman on the television said. "My boyfriend Terence broke up with me a couple of weeks ago. He called one of those sex psychologists. I'm at home and I get this phone call from my friend, Brenda. 'Evie, she says, turn on the radio. Your boyfriend is breaking up with you.'"

Evie took another bite of the Grape Nuts pie Phil had made. Her roommates weren't home for a change; they'd gone to The Water Bar in the lower Haight to drink five dollar bottles imported from Danish springs. Evie had promised to tape her show for them, but she was upset that they hadn't stayed home with her, so she was taping over the episode of *Thirtysomething* where Gary dies.

"So I decided," the woman on the TV said, "if my boyfriend can dump me on the radio, then I can ask him back on television." TV Evie looked straight at flesh and blood Evie.

"Terence, I miss you. I neeeed you."

The audience was laughing, laughing at this woman onstage, this woman who looked and acted so much like Evie but really,

Paul S. Brownfield

in the final analysis, was not. The real Evie lived in a studio apartment, with a Murphy bed and imaginary roommates, and all sorts of strange things stuck to her bathroom wall. The real Evie was embarrassed and saddened now, and wanted to change the channel, just point the remote control at the television and replace herself with a movie of the week.

"I'm begging you, Terence," the comic repeated, and there were more laughs from the audience, and a wry smile from TV Evie, while the real Evie wept, wept because she so admired this comic's pluck, the strength of character that got her up onstage, in spite of everything. The defiant little girl in a pink dress, belting "I'm A Little Tea Cup" to all those half-crazed relatives, bloated and applauding, wanting more.

In an instant, university president Earl Bullock realized his school had a brain-drain problem of staggering proportions.

Paul S. Brownfield lives in Cambridge. This is his first published story.

NO PERMANENT BAD THING / *Kim Edwards*

ONE THING I KNOW for true: I want to touch him. I push my hands into my pockets, fists against my hipbones, so they do not move to feel his arm, his back, rub the nape of his neck. I look at him for too long, and when he sees me, I look away, but not before I see him smile.

We are standing under the bridge at Damascus. This is not the bridge whispered about by the grade nine cheerleaders in third period biology, where they come to rumple their clothes and moan and frustrate themselves and their boyfriends. This is the other bridge, the bridge by the old train bridge, the bridge where he comes with my brother and their crew, and they light fires and talk and act stupidly and take off their clothes and sail out onto the river in the rowboat that they dock in the bushes when they leave.

We are standing by the place where the ridge comes into the ground. Because I need to touch something, I turn to the cement and put my fingers where my brother has spray painted his name in big red letters, and just off to the side, I see another name, his. I turn to see if he is watching what I do, and when I see that he is not, I touch the name, painted small and concentrated. I feel the letters with my fingertips, I stroke them slowly, each one by itself, alone. I write over them with my finger, then I push my palm hard against them. I push them flat into the concrete, to make sure they will stay.

This is a place for boys, and I should maybe not be here. This is a boy place where boys sometimes bring girls and get the girls naked and make the girls laugh, and I am maybe too young to be here; this is only the second summer I have given any real thought to sex. I am thinking about it now, but in my loose shorts, T-shirt and high-tops, I may not be dressed right for mating purposes. I have not curled my hair or applied make-up, and there is a scab on my knee where I cut myself shaving.

I know why I want to be here. I want to be here with him, to kiss him and touch him and let him touch me. I want to listen to him talk and tell me all his secrets and hear him say my name sweet-like, and he would realize that I am more than just good at shooting hoops and being a smartass, that I am . . . more. I know why I am here: I am here because of the paint. He says he has some painting to do at the bridge, and I say that dad has some paint left over from when he and my brother painted the house earlier in the summer and he is welcome to it. So, I give him the paint, and he brings me to the bridge.

Johnny says, The water's low, we could walk out, but let's get the boat.

I say, okay.

I hold the can of paint while he drags the boat from the bushes. Johnny pulls the boat to the water. We load the boat with the paint, a roller pan, a paint roller and an extension handle, along with a six pack of cola, all of which we have taken from the bed of Johnny's Isuzu pickup. I step in and Johnny pushes off. He picks a blanket up from the floor of the boat. I know it's from my mother's hall closet, brought here by my brother.

Simon's contribution to romance on the river, says Johnny. He smiles, a white-tooth smile that I see real good because of the full, big, white, whole moon pushing light from the sky down on the river and shining back up again, big whole moon smiling pretty at its own reflection and making soft light for Johnny and me.

We're going out to the middle, Johnny says. That's where the paint job needs to be done.

Okay, I say.

Okay, says Johnny, and I can see he is smiling at how I am so agreeable, and I think about splashing some water on him but decide that is maybe too girl of a thing to do, so I don't do it. Instead, I put my hand in the water and let the river move against it. I know the color of the water here. It is dry-leaf brown. But that is the color of the river in the daylight, that is the dry-leaf brown color of the sun. Under the big whole moon, the water is deep dream color. The water is no color at all, but the color shining off it from moon and bridge light spilling and from the light off the faces of Johnny and me, and behind all that, the water is just no color, and I put my hand into it, and my hand disappears like through Alice's looking glass, and I pull my hand back out and watch the water drip off it and think that I am happy because I am here alone with Johnny, and if I have to fall through the looking glass to stay this way, that is fine with me.

Johnny rows to the middle of the river and puts the oars to

rest. He picks up the colas, opens one and hands it to me and then opens another for himself. The boat moves only small bits. The water is late summer shallow, and the current is slight.

I like it here, says Johnny.

Me too, I say.

Has Simon brought you here before?

No. This is my maiden voyage, I say, so to speak.

So to speak, says Johnny. I blush at the innuendo and look to the sky for something to say, something that will make Johnny know how much it means to me just to talk to him, how much I want to touch him, just float here for a while and touch his leg, my hand on his thigh, just a soft touch, just a touch to know that he is there, near. He would not have to speak. Would not have to say anything. He would not have to make any promises or tell any lies or exaggerate any stories. He could just be there with me and my hand on his thigh, and the boat would drift slightly, just bit by bit, slowly to the shore until we banked, and then we could climb out onto the shore, and he would drive me home.

Johnny picks up the oars and begins to row again. He pulls the boat alongside one of the bridge's support piers. He pushes one of the oars down into the riverbed and says to me, Keep this pushed out so that the boat holds steady against the pier, okay?

Aye, captain, I say.

Johnny grins, opening the paint and pouring some into the pan. You're a fine first mate, Denny, he says. He hooks the paint roller onto the extension handle and stands up in the boat.

Hold her steady there, says Johnny, and he dips the roller into the pan of paint and lifts it over his head up high to a place on the concrete pier that says JOHNNY LOVES KYRA, and he paints until the pier says only LOVES KYRA and the job is done.

Johnny sits back down, unhooks the roller from the handle, pours the extra paint from the pan back into the can, closes the lid on the can and says, Not too painful.

Not too, I say.

Johnny looks close to sad, so I take up the oars and paddle real slow and a little uneven as I am not so practiced in rowboat technique. When we are away from the pier, I stop rowing and pick up two colas. I open one for Johnny and then one for myself.

Thanks, Johnny says. And we sit and listen to the sound of a car passing overhead on the bridge, and off on the shore crickets are at work in the woods, creaking each other's names.

I hold my cola with both hands and roll it between my palms. It feels good to have something there to touch, to keep my hands busy, to keep them to themselves.

What did you say to her, I ask Johnny, in the quiet times?

Like when?

Like, after you made love. What did you talk about?

I don't know. Different things. Sometimes we would talk about the sex we just had. Sometimes, if it was in the afternoon, we would just talk about, you know, whatever we were going to go ahead and do. Sometimes we would talk about intimacy. About degrees of intimacy.

Like what?

Like, why our relationship was different from any relationship we had with anyone else.

What did you decide?

She decided, says Johnny, that she had never shared herself with anyone like she had shared herself with me. That I knew her better than anyone.

And you?

I have not decided, says Johnny. There are . . .

So many people, I say.

Yes, says Johnny.

Even Simon, I say.

Johnny smiles. Even Simon, he says, knows me so well.

Not to mention, I say, Laura and Chris and Heather and, wait, I say, who was it before Heather? Kendall, is that right, or was she one of Simon's?

I believe, Johnny says, that Kendall loved both Simon and me equally but probably for different reasons.

Oh, I say, of course. She no doubt loved Simon for his fine mind and you for your ability to burp hello.

No doubt, Johnny says and then he starts to laugh. His laugh gets big real quick, and I feel the boat shake with the sound of it. His laugh gets big and happy, and all that sad-eye-Johnny look is gone for complete from his eyes, and he shakes up his cola and aims it right at me and starts squirting me in a cola shower so I rock the boat hard, and he is grabbing to keep paint and roller and pan and handle and oars all on board and forgetting to hold on for himself and out he goes. Johnny through the looking glass. He is under water and then up through the looking glass again and he grabs me up out of the boat and throws me in and I'm laughing big and hard too so that I breathe in water and think I am either going to die now from bad poison water or break open a lung from laughing so big. I fall back on my butt into the water and sit until the laughter starts to quiet nice to giggles.

And I, watching, want to move closer. I want to move right up and take his hair in my hand and pull his head back and push my mouth on his mouth and keep my eyes open to see if he keeps his eyes open or closes them, to see what his brows are doing and watch how he is breathing, to see if his forehead wrinkles and where he will put his hands. I want to suck his tongue into my mouth, and all those words deep down in Johnny's throat, straight from Johnny's heart would come up like gas through a siphon and pour into me and my tongue, my words into him, straight from inside down deep-heart, straight from Johnny into me and me into Johnny.

And Johnny stands up and holds out his hand, and I want him to take me by the arms. One Johnny hand on either of my arms and just push into me hard or soft or slow or fast or however he would want, I wouldn't mind. Johnny knows more about such things than I do, and I am wanting him to pull me so bad that I close my eyes for just a minute and let it happen to me because if I do not let it happen now, here in the looking glass wet, I do not know when I will be at such a place again and I do not know if Johnny will be there with me. I close my eyes just for a minute, and I open them and Johnny's hand is closer now and his smile is sweet, light and pretty on the looking glass wet. It shines back up at me from below and down on me from above, and I take Johnny's hand and he pulls me up.

We walk the boat back to the bank. My high tops being sucked into the mud of the riverbed, I high-step to free them and then up out of the water onto the shore. We pull the boat up, and Johnny takes out the blanket and spreads it on the ground and says, Let's dry off a little. I'll build a fire.

Okay, I say. So he starts to gather up some branches and dritwood and I pick up a stick here and there and add it to the pile. I look up to the ridge when a truck goes over and watch its headlights loom and disappear. I look at Johnny. He has been my brother's friend since forever. Since forever Johnny has been in my life. I remember it was Johnny who helped Simon dig the grave out under the box elder tree, the grave for the first cat, Tom. Johnny stood quiet and good while we said a prayer and wrapped Tom in my own baby blanket, and Johnny is the one who put the first dirt on the grave because Simon was biting his lip too hard to move. Johnny is the one who played tin can cobble on late summer nights after our parents were in the house with the TV talking, and Johnny always came to kick the can and set me free, and we ran and hid way back in the field behind the house in the tall grass where Johnny's brother and my brother could not find us so good. And when Mama and Simon were in the car wreck, it was at Johnny's house I stayed while dad was at the hospital, and it was in Johnny's room I slept, quiet in his sleeping bag after he played his records for me and let me win at video games.

After this summer, things will change. Simon and Johnny will not be in the halls at school, and my friends will not swoon and say how sweet my brother is and what a nice walk he has, and I am so lucky because I live in a house with him, and he brings all those friends home too. This is the last summer before Johnny leaves. I know he is going, I have heard him talk.

I sit down on the blanket and watch as Johnny starts the fire. I untie my shoes and put them close to the flames.

Looks like you could use a new pair of All Stars, says Johnny.

I push one of the high tops with my foot and say, Yeah. New shoes, new clothes, new hair. Maybe I'll get a perm.

Don't do that, says Johnny.

I feel a smile spread all warm across my face.

I like your hair the way it is, Johnny says.

Washed in toxic river water? I ask.

Especially washed in river water, he says.

I reach and push my wet hair up from my forehead. I push it back behind my ear, combing it with my fingers. I reach and push Johnny's hair out of his face, up over his forehead. He smiles good and lets me touch him, and I push my fingers through his hair, over his head, down past his neck and squeeze his hair long to his back, squeeze it in my hand and wring the water from it. I hold Johnny's long hair in my hand, thick and wet, and then I let go.

Johnny pokes at the fire, and I lean back on my elbows and look up at the stars and think about all the wishes I have made there and how in the last year Johnny has been included in so many wishes, and I say to Johnny, because I want to know what he will say back, because I want to know if I should be as scared sometimes as I am I say, Sometimes I think I am doing this whole girl thing all wrong.

How? Johnny asks.

Like, I don't wear the right clothes or have the right hair, and I don't giggle enough, and I don't know how to use a curling iron and, you know, stuff like that.

That's just stuff, says Johnny. I think you're doing the girl thing exactly right.

Yeah?

Yeah.

I feel my stomach get excited, and my breathing is just quick enough that I know my heart is pumping extra flows of red blood stuff, putting all my nerve endings on alert, and getting me ready to tingle like a tingle you get when you are waiting for someone to touch you because you know the touch is only inches away, and it is like you, tingle—feel it even before the actual hand-on-skin contact is made.

I lay back on the blanket and I say to Johnny, You like me, a lot, right?

Yes.

I keep my face looking up at the sky and I try to figure where the big dipper and the little dipper are, the mama and her bear cub, and I can never figure the sky. Simon can always point them out. He can see the constellations, but I can never find them on my own. It is all blinking, shining lights to me, all stars, each one as nice as the next, all special, all wishes whispered up to the sky.

If I stay real still, if I do not move, he will touch me. If I stay quiet and say nothing, he will reach a hand over and touch my arm and maybe face-lean into me and look in my eyes and maybe that look, that one look where his eyes take the place of the stars and I look into his face, maybe in that look, he will fall in love with me. If I stay still and wait for the touch, the look. My heart is moving quick now while I wait to feel if Johnny will touch me, and he does.

Johnny touches my hair. He holds a strand of my hair up, and then lets it fall over my eye, my nose.

You're a strange kid, says Johnny.

I look at him and say, think you could ever fall in love with a strange kid?

Sure, sometime.

Sometime?

Not now.

Why not now? Because I'm too young?

No, says Johnny, because I am too young.

Too young to fall in love?

Mmmhmm.

But, what about Kyra? Weren't you in love with her?

No, says Johnny. He looks at me and grins a grin like I know what he is going to say and before he says it, I do. He says, And I wasn't in love with Laura or Chris or Heather or even Kendall either.

What about Simon? I ask because I am a smartass, because Johnny has come to expect these questions from me, because I like Johnny a lot, and I want to make him talk. You love Simon don't you?

Simon, he says, is another thing all together. Simon, says Johnny, Simon is . . .

A fucking toad, I say.

A fucking toad, says Johnny. But, he's still my best friend in the whole world.

And you love him.

And I love him.

Because who else would put up with you?

No one, except my mom, says Johnny, and, maybe, Johnny says, you.

Maybe me, I say.

Johnny stands and says, Come on. Let's go on the train bridge.

I follow him up the embankment to where the train tracks come off the ground and start the ridge over the river. Johnny climbs over the barrier put in place by the train company, past the NO TRESPASSING signs and onto the train bridge. He watches as I follow behind him. He watches until I am over the barrier and onto the bridge with him. Then we walk, from tie to tie, the wood sometimes soft, but not yet rotten, beneath our feet. The river is far below here and moon shines its surface up at us on the bridge. Johnny walks ahead, but not too far. He slow-walks some and keeps an eye half on me to quick grab me if I slip, but he walks ahead because he knows that I do not want to need him to help me walk on the bridge. I do not want him to think I am too scared and Johnny knows this, so he slow-walks just ahead of me. Sometimes there is a missing tie, and the step is a bigger leg stretch, and Johnny waits to make sure I do all right over the extra gap, but this only happens twice, and we move on out to the middle of the bridge. There, Johnny slides himself down and sits on a tie, one leg hangs down to the river, the other bent in front of him, against another tie. I sit down on this tie, the tie where Johnny's foot is at rest.

Down the river, I can see the city lights and harbor lights clear out to the big lake. And the big lake is like another sky far out to the east where sky and lake are the same color, and I cannot see where the line is between them. But the lights are far off and just look like closer stars, and I cannot see any constellations in these stars either, just more blinking, shining lights to make wishes on.

Johnny's hair moves to kiss his face in the breeze that comes down the river from off the lake. His hair covers his eyes and back again and wraps sweet around his cheeks and makes him dark against the sky.

I think of feeling Johnny close. I think of being breathing close to him, feeling him breathing and me breathing the same air and his air out into me and mine to him. I think of talking to him forever and telling him all my secrets when I know myself what my secrets are. I think of running my tongue softly into his ear to taste what he hears when I speak and know if what he hears is what I say or maybe more, what I meant, what I want.

I think of Johnny going away and, when he is old enough, calling me on the phone. He will say something simple, just what he means. He will say, Denny, come see me. Come be where I am. And, if I am still old enough, I will go. I think of going to where Johnny will be, and there his hair will still be long, kissing his face and my hair will move to cover his head, and we could comb our hair together with the brush of our fingers.

I smile at Johnny as he pushes back his hair in the lake river breeze.

Do you think you'll fall in love someday? I ask Johnny.

He smiles at me and rubs a hand along his thigh. I think, says Johnny, that I just may do that.

Sure you will, I say.

You're sure of that, huh?

Yes, I say. I am sure.

How about you? Johnny asks. Are you going to fall in love someday?

Yes, I say.

Johnny pulls himself up and reaches his hand for mine. I give him my hand, and he squeezes it and steps onto the tie I am on and warm-slides his arm through my arm and then over my shoulder and we cross back over the bridge and onto the shore.

Johnny puts dirt on the fire, and we put all the paint supplies in the back of his truck, and Johnny says, Wait a second.

He pulls out the paint can and a brush from his truck and says, Hey, Denny, you have to leave your mark.

So I go to the cement where the bridge comes into the ground, and I paint my name, there just beside my brother's name, just next to Johnny's name. I make my mark.

The Angels of Death and Taxes do lunch.

Kim Edwards lives in Ohio and is at work on her first novel.

UNCLE ROY'S PEARL HARBOR HOT DOGS
/ *Walter McDonald*

Old Uncle Roy wore American flags
for a topcoat, a hat made of owls'
and eagles' feathers. Ringing a bell downtown
all day, he rolled an oblong hot-dog stand,
shaped like a bomb in World War II.

He daubed white stars and stripes
gaudy and rippling. He bent the tin
and fastened it with screws, live coals inside
to warm the buns and wieners.
Before the war, he pedaled aimlessly around,

without a family, no dog, one eye wobbling
along in traffic, the other laughing.
He waved at everyone and most of us
waved back, uncle of all in name only.
After Pearl Harbor, we saw him on foot,

dragging long sheets of tin down alleys.
One day there he was, big bomb of hot dogs
and Uncle Roy in flags, yelling, "Dogs!
Beat Hitler with a dog!" Who taught him
what to charge we never learned,

maybe angels he heard on Sundays—a dime
for himself, a dime for war bonds.
Wheels wobbled under the load
as he shoved our favorite food downtown,
ringing, ringing the bell.

MOUNDS AT ESTACADO / *Walter McDonald*

Hawks alone could have loved it
before pumps and irrigation, flat plains
of cactus. Wolves caught rabbits
stampeded by buffalos, miles between water holes.

Grandfather rode a bouncing wagon here,
his wife worn out by Amarillo, five children
squalling for meat, for water. He fed them
rabbits and prairie dogs. My daddy said the meat

was stringy, needing no salt. The last buffalo
was penned at Jake Smith's trading post.
Granddaddy pitched a tent which blew away,
West Texas sandstorms worse than Iowa winters,

ashes from heaven. He buried his wife that year
and took a Quaker maiden from Estacado.
She bore him four more boys and buried him
herself in Estacado, the only Quaker left.

All others rolled their wagons to the gulf,
even her parents. I've seen some cousins
in Galveston, held in my hand their hands.
They watched me as if I were the ghost,

survivor of sandstorms they carry as folk tales,
one great crazy aunt who stayed on the plains
like Lot's wife. I've touched the stone she turned to
on Granddaddy's plot in Estacado,

a graveyard bordered by barbed wires,
ghost town surrounded by pastures,
cows and romping calves in all directions,
bumblebees roaming the miles of cactus.

THE SIGNS OF PRAIRIE RATTLERS
/ Walter McDonald

The days of rattlesnake chili are back,
hulls and jalapeños the way to make eye vessels bleed.
This may be the year of the snake, fat rattlers
on every trail. All day in the saddle
I see jackrabbits to wide horizons. Out here,

the eyes don't believe in signs. We shove sticks down
to make mad rattlers strike, crush their tails
in chili and jalapeños and let their threats be empty.
Not one more rattle can save them from the fire.
I never believed the claims of snake handlers

in carnivals and church. I've heard mad preachers
claim this sand is the same as Bible deserts.
They quoted Moses with serpents impaled on poles.
Watch signs, they warned with spitting tongues—
coyotes trying to mate with your dogs at noon,

a mirage that shimmers at dawn, owls that dive
and pluck snake eyes like grapes.
They prophesied a thousand years of peace.
At times, after the madness of Saigon,
I've found rattlers mangled at dawn,

ripped open but only the skull devoured,
eyeless in Gaza. I've seen coyotes at noon
lame in the hip and starving, risking the ranch
in daylight. I've cut a window in my wall
to save barn owls from cats. My rafters

are an ark for owls. I have faith
in most home remedies—hard work
and red-eyed chili and homespun love.
Prophets in revival tents when I was five
are dead or mumbling in retirement homes.

I've seen them preaching to themselves in shawls
in rocking chairs they haven't the power to move.
I've seen their stares, starved for faith
in more than serpents, their folded hands,
their blinking, hollow eyes.

RIGGING THE WINDMILL / *Walter McDonald*

Now it begins, oaks spinning autumn
into gold. What enters my hand is old
and dented, my father's oil can.
Oiling the blades, I back to the edge
and watch them spin. Out pumps

the same sweet water from the pipe.
I squirt another drop for luck
and grab the ladder, swing out one leg
and glance around—the flat backs
of Herefords trudging to the trough,

trees thick as a windbreak, the glint
of neighbors' windmills. Bracing
with one stiff hand, I twist the wrench
as if all cattle on the plains
depended on it. Without a breeze,

we'd all be stranded without a gourd of water.
We take beguiling skies for granted
on the plains, the hands we hold from habit.
Most hours, we ignore the clatter of steel
on steel, each other's steady breath,

the mystery of wells. No matter where we've been,
it's home. Tonight, we'll rock
on the porch swing, hearing the bawl
of a calf, a dog barking a mile away,
the whirring blades.

UNCLE PHILIP AND THE ENDLESS NAMES
/ *Walter McDonald*

Uncle Philip hated work, walked off a dozen jobs
before thirty. Wide jaw, sharp teeth, he sported
a wiry moustache and smoked, believed the sisters
from Bovina who called him handsome.
He remembered their names when he was eighty.

His mother died when he was ten,
five years before he enlisted. Never mind the war,
the Kaiser's army of millions. Uncle Philip
won it over and over, his doubled fists like tanks.
Smoking, he coughed what he claimed

was mustard gas, the trenches of France
what killed him. He lingered sixty years
with cigars, his quarrel with the war
all that saved him from steady work,
the pension he never got stuck in his craw

like a wound. I remember the tilt of his cap
in pictures, a Texas doughboy in Paris,
caught with some girl he never saw again.
He taught me to toss a hook between logs
in the shallows, how to find bass in a dozen lakes.

He taught me to drive, slouched in his truck and
    smoking,
coaxed me to shift those gears like butter, don't lean
into turns but trust them, believing all eighteen wheels
would follow. When I glanced back in the mirror,
they followed. I remember his eyes in the rest home.

I followed his stare to the ceiling,
the shapeless water stains. Pointing,
he called forgotten names like a roll call,
soldiers I'd only heard of,
girls from Bovina, *Mother, Mother*.

HAWKS IN AUGUST / *Walter McDonald*

All summer we brush the dust,
proof of people who worshipped
the same tornado sky we worship,
a scraping tool, an arrowhead,

a perfect skull. The smell of cactus
rises in thermals, drifts east
and turns to clouds by sundown,
dry as antlers on walls of honky-tonk cafes.

The only rain for months was rumor.
Again in the east, dark clouds
like flints no lightning strikes
to make sweet water fall.

Without a flood, this may be the year
of the buzzard. We tag the bones
of wolves under oaks Quakers planted
in 1880, seeking pastures of heaven.

We wonder what they found that summer,
huddled in dug-outs to survive
the sandstorms. They stayed two years
before most rolled wagons

to Galveston. Coronado rode here
four centuries ago, defying Comanches
for gold, his soldiers grumbling,
stumbling beside their stallions.

We breathe the dust of their wandering.
Who could have known we'd find bones
miles from mountains, buried with flints
ten thousand years? Hawks keep watch

from above, hoping for anything
to hop into sunlight. They bank

dark wings and glide in spirals
over fields so parched they stare.

Walter McDonald has published several books of poems, including *Night Landings* and *The Digs in Escondido Canyon*.

TAMING MONSTERS/ *Tricia Tunstall*

T HERE IS A SIGN, hand-lettered on red construction paper, on her son's bedroom door. It says: NO MONSTERS CAN COME HERE. THAT'S THE LAW.

Her son dictated the words to her at bedtime one night. He watched, his wet lips parted, as she wrote the sign and taped it up. Later, getting into bed, he clung to her. "Mommy," he whispered, "can monsters read?"

She reads, these days, books on child development, combing the indexes for FEARS, NIGHTTIME or MONSTERS, FEAR OF. She knows from these books that four-year-olds are commonly afraid of imaginary beings. She understands that the fears are normal and will pass. "Yes," she tells her son, "monsters can read."

Her husband does not approve of this. He says that by going along with the fantasies she is reinforcing them. "Robbie," he says to his son, "there are no monsters. Right?"

"Right," says Robbie.

"Say it, Robbie. Say 'There are no monsters, not in New York, not anywhere.'"

"There's no monsters in New York," says Robbie, bored.

"Or anywhere."

"Anywhere."

They have this conversation at dinner one night. After dinner, Robbie will not put on his pajamas until she moves the sign lower on the door. "They can't see it so high up," he tells her. The monsters, it seems, are just about as tall as Robbie.

She reads the books on child development on the subway, on her way to work. She teaches English to private students, mostly Japanese businessmen who want to improve their knowledge of the vernacular. She visits their offices for one-hour sessions; they close their doors, offer her tea, ask her questions. "What does it mean, 'wiped out'?" they say. "What does it mean, 'get down'?" She feels tremendous next to them, these small spruce flat-haired gentlemen who smell of scents with woodland names. She feels puff-haired, fat-kneed; her hands look too large for her pen. But she likes the work. It gives her a sense of being useful, necessary to the world's comings and goings. The gentlemen pay her well, do their homework, correct their own grammar with beseeching looks. They buy paperback novels in drugstores. "What does it mean, 'sugar daddy'?"

One of her students has a friend who wants lessons. "He wants a lot lessons," says the student.

"He wants lessons a lot," she corrects him.

He shakes his head. "He wants a lot lessons. He has a lot money."

It is a small but potent thrill, being recommended, being sought. With the student acting as intermediary, she makes an appointment with the friend. On the morning of the appointment her son bursts uncharacteristically into tears when she leaves him at nursery school. "Mommy, I have to pee," he wails, "stay till I pee!" The panic in his voice frightens her. She stands next to him at the little toilet, waiting. Now he is relaxed, conversational. "You have to *shake* it, see?" he tells her.

The address she has been given is north of the financial district, in Soho. As she goes up the subway steps the sun is white, polished, almost wet-looking. She wishes she knew some Japanese. She has asked several of the businessmen to teach her a few words, but they always smile and tell her, "It's very difficult, Japanese." They are the bilingual ones, not she; they want to keep it that way.

She arrives at a low cast-iron building, its facade blackened by decades of fumes, its windows covered with bars. A man lies on the stoop sleeping, clutching a single running shoe like a teddy bear. She steps around him and rings the bell.

There is silence for a long time. The man sleeping behind her stirs slightly, sings in his sleep. The night before her son had wakened over and over, sobbing. "I can't tell you," he had gasped when she asked what he had been dreaming. "I need some water. I'm cold. Just stay with me *one minute* and *that's it*," he promised, lying with desperate sincerity. She had finally fetched her pillow from the bed where her husband lay, and gone to sleep on her son's floor. In the morning she had wakened with circles on her cheek, the imprint of a stray Duplo block.

The door opens suddenly and she faces a large man, taller and darker-skinned than her other students, and probably younger. He holds out his hand and says what might be his name, then leads her down a long hall and up a flight of iron stairs. "My studio," he tells her as he opens a door into a large room, flooded with hard-boiled light from huge windows facing the street. His accent is faintly British, his tee shirt sleeveless. The muscles in his arms are outlined in black ink.

She looks around the loft. Canvases are everywhere, hung from the ceiling, on the walls, the supporting beams. They are meticulous reproductions of the kind of pictures of food that are displayed in Burger King or McDonald's: huge burgers coiffed with lettuce and tomatoes, tall glasses of sweating soda, fried fish cakes surrounded by curly french fries. The reproductions are perfect, the colors faithful; they differ from the real thing only in size, as the smallest of them is at least ten feet square. "You are an artist," she says, enunciating the words as if the lesson has already begun.

"Yes," he says. "You want tea?"

He wants to talk about food. As the tea water heats he walks around the loft, pointing. "Meat balls," she pronounces carefully. "Cole slaw." He repeats the words after her; their contours are blurred by his Japanese accent, resharpened with the British tinge in his speech. "Big Mac," she says.

He looks joyful. "Big Mac!" he cries, gazing at his picture, "Big Mac!"

Over a cup of black, leaf-strewn tea she attempts conversation. It becomes clear that his English is primitive, and she suggests they work on some grammar, learn a few verbs. "To what avail?" he asks politely. Where could he have learned that? He does not know the words for spoon, cup, sugar. "To what avail?"

"So you can be comfortable with the language," she tells him sternly. He smiles, looking skeptical, and stretches his arms above his head. Someone else must have done the etching along his muscles; he could not possibly have managed it himself. She wonders how seriously he takes it; she finds herself disapproving.

She structures an impromptu grammar lesson around his paintings. "The Big Mac *is* on the plate," he repeats. "The french fries *are* on the plate." As midday approaches the colors in the paintings flash with neon fervor. At noon she rises and puts on her coat. His smile is abrupt, tremendous. "Can you come every day?" he asks. She feels proud of his perfect sentence as she shakes her head.

"I have only one morning a week free," she tells him.

"But after mornings?"

"Afternoons," she says. She remembers that he has a lot of money, and wonders if his paintings sell for high prices. She tells him she will think about it, and will call him.

On the subway platform a reggae band is playing. The music reminds her of the Japanese man's paintings; it has the same slick, sweet simplicity. He learned from her with unconditional ease; she feels almost dizzy with competence. But if she works with him in the afternoons she will have to hire someone to pick up Robbie from nursery school and stay with him until she gets home. The thought of this makes her teeth ache. Her romance with Robbie is intricate, passionate, a tightly braided skein of coded messages and solemn pleasures, fights and reconciliations. After several years devoted to learning how to make her angry he has recently acquired the gift of making her laugh: he tells her long soap opera plots about dinosaurs, makes up knock-knock jokes, pulls off her glasses and puts them on his own face upside down. They build Duplo structures together; he is patient with her mistakes. While she makes dinner or does the dishes he puts together puzzles on the kitchen floor and then colors in, with crayons, the spaces on the floor where pieces are missing. He knows she will be furious, and will laugh.

She places an ad in the newspaper for a babysitter, hoping no one will call. They call; dozens call, with accents from all over the hemisphere and some from other hemispheres. Eventually she turns on her answering machine and lets the accents flow as the tape runs. Late at night, when Robbie is asleep, she listens to them, replaying the ones with a lilt in the voice, an edge of humor or confidence. She writes down the phone numbers and calls them back for interviews.

They come, young girls, older women, some with babies in strollers, others with careful makeup. "What is your experience?" she asks them. They have experience; they have references. She doesn't believe a word they say, any of them. They are too slow-moving or too nervous; their English is too broken or their nails too long. She uses the monster sign as a test, and there are many ways to fail. "Isn't that cute!" some say, or, wide-eyed, "Ooo, where's the monster?" which is no better than "A big boy like you afraid of monsters?" She rules these out instantly, with a shiver of relief each time. Some of them simply ignore the sign. She is not sure if this disqualifies them or not. Her son spends the interviews with his face in her lap, making clear the enormity of his injury. If he would only give a sign, raise his head for one of them, she could choose. She sighs, laces her fingers through his hair. "I'll let you know," she says.

She wakes in the middle of the night, her heart beating as though she has been caught in a crime. She nudges her husband. "They're awful," she tells him, half-accusingly.

He rolls over. "Honey, what are you looking for? Mary Poppins? Katie Nana?"

"God forbid," she says. "Mary Poppins was a punitive bitch. Katie Nana let those kids get stolen."

"Nobody's good enough for you," he says. "All we need is a nice girl. Other people get nice girls. Just get somebody. If it doesn't work out you can fire her. You don't have to do this job, you know," he added. "Do what makes you happy." He is asleep.

The next day she calls the painter to tell him she will not be able to work with him. "You have dialed a non-working number," says a recording. She stares at her scrap of paper; the numbers are in his handwriting. They are elegant, assured. She can't guess which is likeliest to be wrong.

A girl comes that afternoon, a girl with a Brooklyn accent and recently pink hair. She says she is in night school, studying word processing. Her fingernails are bitten all the way down. She takes off her sunglasses and stares at the back of Robbie's buried head. "Are you gonna talk to me or what?" she says. Startled, Robbie lifts his face slightly and peeks at her. She puts her sunglasses back on upside down. Robbie laughs.

In the Soho loft she and the Japanese painter decide she will call him George. She is embarrassed at her inability to say, or even hear, his Japanese name, but he doesn't seem to mind. "George," he repeats, making it two syllables. He likes it. "You are easy. Anne."

She has brought a grammar book. "It is easy," she tells him, seizing on his word. They turn to the first dialogue in the book. "I am going for a walk." "May I come with you?" "If you like." "That is a pretty dress." Large line drawings depict the conversationalists, a teenaged girl and boy, she with schoolbooks pressed against her chest, he with a backwards baseball cap. "May I go with you?" muses George, gazing at the picture. "May I go with you?" He glances up suddenly. "More food, okay?" he says gently.

She closes the book, keeping her fingers in to mark the page. She loves the food, but isn't sure it is a serious way to teach English. He has gotten out more paintings, ones she didn't see the first time. These are from earlier strata of the American dining record: malted milkshakes, pepper steaks, banana splits. The colors are lurid. It takes George several tries to learn "banana split." When

Tricia Tunstall

he finally pronounces it he is elated. He throws open a window and yells it to the street below. "You want food?" he asks, and she understands that it is lunch he is talking about this time, and that he has experienced her words as a gift.

He makes cellophane noodles. Shitake mushrooms lie across the top like wilted orchids. She stares; it would make a spectacular painting. "George," she asks, "have you ever eaten the food you paint?"

He gazes at her as the words click in, one by one, then shakes his head silently; either he does not know the words to justify this or is aware he doesn't need to. The American foods, she thinks, are his monsters; painting, he tames them. They eat lunch; she asks him how to say "noodles" in Japanese. He teaches her the words for noodles, chopsticks, mushrooms, and paint. He teaches her to say, "May I go with you?"

Riding home on the subway, she reads: if your four-year-old develops acute and irrational fears, your best bet is not to introduce any changes in his life, and spend some extra time with him. She arrives home to find the apartment empty, Robbie's toys neat on the shelves. She takes off her coat and washes five carrots before she calls the police.

The door opens as she dials and Robbie wanders in, followed by the babysitter, whose name she cannot remember. He has a smear of chocolate on one cheek, a fistful of crushed leaves. "Hi, Mommy," he says, "I brought you some nature." He lays the leaves in her lap and then turns to his babysitter, who stands slouching, her hands in the back pockets of her jeans, behind him. "Let's go play, Sarah," he says to her, confident, casual.

"She's a nice girl," she tells her husband that night. "I think she'll be good for him."

"Maybe she'll manage to get rid of that monster sign," says her husband, only partly teasing.

That night she wakes up just before Robbie starts to cry. The silence feels like a crucial mistake, a clue. Then the wail rises, and she runs to him, her husband behind her this time because the cry is piercing, more a scream than a sob. She scoops up her son. "What is it?" she calls, her hands on his cheeks. "What is scary?"

"You say it, Mommy," he stammers, "I can't say it."

"Sweetie, is it Sarah?" she says, almost eagerly.

He blinks at her, his face drenched. "Who's Sarah?" he asks. A new cycle of sobs grips him. "The sign, the sign is down," he wails.

She goes to his doorway, turns on the hall light. "See, Robbie, the sign is still here," she says. He is crouched behind his father, who is sitting on the bed. She ignores the look on her husband's face as she reads the sign very slowly, as though she were reading it to the Japanese painter, aloud to her son. As she reads she understands that she herself is comforted by the sign.

In the course of the next few days she and George go out to lunch at a Burger King, a coffee shop, and two McDonald's. He eats, for the first time, the food he has painted; she sees that he doesn't like it much but seems to accept her theory that he will paint it better if he has tasted it. To the accoutrements she finds so offensive—the plastic, the styrofoam, the muzak—he is impervious. She begins ordering cheeseburgers instead of garden salads, remembers to ask for extra ketchup. By the end of the week George has linguistic command of the full menus of every fast food establishment in lower Manhattan. They begin to cook. They make sushi, lasagna, chicken in wine sauce. He can speak of vinaigrette, smoked oysters. One day's lunch often turns up the next day on canvas, the ingredients swollen, vivified. He tells her that since he speaks English with no one else he thinks of the language as one they have made up together, a private mode of communication impenetrable by others. The truth of this excites and troubles her; every detail they add to the sealed world they are making together, every crushed herb and possessive pronoun, is a sharp edge denting the contours of the rest of her life. When she cooks with him she goes barefoot, and the soles of her feet are prismatic with paint stains.

She tries to create leaks, to trail connections between the parts of her life. She tells the businessmen about George's paintings; she talks to the babysitter of the businessmen, to her husband of the babysitter. They listen, from a distance. To George she talks, slowly and carefully, about Robbie. George repeats the names of Robbie's toys; no question, he is a noun man; he needs very few verbs. His joy is in things, their creases, colors, grain. He is dazzled by specificity. "Ghost zapper," she tells him, "proton pak." He writes the words on napkins, in Japanese characters. She tells him finally about the fears. When she explains the word "monsters" he repeats it several times, nods; he seems to grasp the utter specificity of monsters.

When she arrives home in the late afternoons Robbie is always placid, somewhat distant but polite. She wonders if she is imagining that his eyes are slowly acquiring the neutral look of the babysitter's eyes. She wonders if they watch TV; she wonders, more painfully, if they don't, and are spending their time together developing intimate and exclusive rituals which are sillier, or less silly, than her own with him. She watches vigilantly for a sign that he is suffering in some way. But he brings her dirty popsicle sticks from the sidewalks, wrestles with his father before bed. Only at night do the terrors emerge, and more and more often now she wakens before he does and lies in bed waiting for his cry to spring the lock of her own fear.

On the day she sleeps with George she has a picture in her pocket that Robbie has made for her, a crayon drawing of, in his words, a bear in a nighttime cave. A morbid picture, she thought when he gave it to her, a huge bruise of purple and black slashes. His smile was radiant as he told her the title. When she arrives at George's loft she shows him the picture immediately, as if asking for a verdict. He lays it on the table, smoothing out the wrinkles. "Monsters," he says.

They open the grammar book; they have progressed past the courting teenagers and are occupied with a mommy, a daddy, a son and a daughter on a car trip. "We are going north on the highway," says the daddy. "See the fields of wheat," says the daughter. "Fields of wheat," repeats George, with a straight face. The inky lines are gone from his arms, but they have taught her the exact contours of his muscles. His sleeveless shirt is black; his feet beneath the frayed blue jean cuffs are bare. Side by side, they stare together at the drawing of the family seatbelted into their car. Near the open book lies Robbie's desperate picture. When George looks up at her he doesn't move; he is waiting for a word, a noun. "George," she says.

He kisses first one cheek, near her ear, then the other, and only then her mouth. When they stand she remembers how tall he is; they won't fit together unless they lie down, and so he turns away and leads her to the curtain strung up in a corner of the loft. He pulls the curtain aside and gestures to her formally, as though he is holding open a car door. She sits on the mattress and he draws the curtain shut before he lies beside her and pulls her down to him. She closes her eyes, then opens them again; the sparseness of their mutual vocabulary makes looking imperative. His hands on her body are paint-flecked, like her feet. Above his bent head a cheeseburger shimmers in a tender spill of light.

On the way home, in the subway, she does not sit down. She grips the pole in one hand, her child development book in the other. The mattress behind the curtain had been white and wide, as wide as the fields of wheat that had, she thinks absurdly, been the proximate cause. What the actual cause had been she cannot begin to guess; she is amazed at the scale of what has happened and at the specificity, the level of detail of sunlight and skin, of which it was composed. She remembers she has promised Robbie a new set of Tinkertoys; he wants to build a laser gun to zap monsters. They have planned exactly how to construct it. She wonders if she has betrayed Robbie because of his new romance. Or did her betrayal come first; did Robbie understand it before she did? Her husband's name passes through her mind, and she lets it go; she cannot find a way to think about him just now.

At her door she finds a key in the lock; the babysitter has left it there by mistake. She turns the key and goes in. Robbie and Sarah are sitting on the kitchen floor; he has tied a complicated knot in the strings of his raincoat hood and Sarah is bent toward him, fussing with the knot. They look up wordlessly when she says hello.

She pulls Robbie's folded picture from her pocket, overwhelmed with the desire to confess. "I showed your picture to a friend of mine, a painter," she tells Robbie. His eyes narrow. "My friend liked it," she adds, and then she is on her knees with her face in Robbie's neck. He smells of rain and peanut butter. She is aware that Sarah is staring at her, but Sarah is implicated now, part of a geometry she has helped, however unwittingly, to create; she can see as much as she cares to. Robbie pulls away. "Mommy, can I have gum?" he says. "Sarah has gum."

"Yes," she says. He turns away from her, back to Sarah and lifts his small chin. She bends over him once more and the knot gives; the raincoat slides off, and he leaps, released, as he runs down the hall to his room.

Tricia Tunstall has published a number of short stories and freelance articles.

LUCK BE A LADY!/ *Anthony Caputi*

HE COULD NEVER decide if he was a gambler pretending to be an accountant or an accountant pretending to be a gambler. To be a gambler you had to make your living by betting, and he didn't. To be an accountant you were supposed to be a model of pecuniary conservatism, and he wasn't. Most of his friends thought the scale tipped in favor of accountant. Unlike most gamblers he had never had great swings of fortune, from storybook winnings to losses taking you over your head into debt, and like an accountant he was careful, cautious even—too cautious, some might say, to be a gambler. But he didn't agree. In fact, he saw no great distance between the two, particularly if you excluded from gambling the games of pure chance. His favorite games, poker and horse racing, were affairs of the mind, after all, exercises in calculation, like accountancy, games to be won by the judicious. Oh, he was familiar with those who thought differently, those bright-eyed occasional players who were all zany superstition, who now and then had staggering successes, but who lost most of the time, griping all the way about bad luck, sometimes punching out door panels and abusing their girl friends. But the players he admired were smart, shrewd assessors of probability, instinctive card-counters, ingenious readers of the *Racing Form*, and canny judges of character and fitness. They were the players who usually won.

What set him off from these good players was that they were often lucky—or so he thought. In the Tuesday and Friday poker games the golden cards fell to them with heart-tightening frequency, straights and three-of-a-kind, flushes and full boats, and even paltry pairs when such were sufficient to win. To them at the racetrack fell the majority of photo finishes and foul claims. When a horse went wide, it was usually to let theirs sneak through on the rail to a tight victory. When a jockey lost his whip, or a horse stumbled coming out of the gate, or a horse ran greenly and interfered with others, it was often to make the difference that enabled them to win. Over months and years he looked on in silence, bemused, sometimes spellbound, as if observing the conclusion of some magical romance. Of course even they called it luck as they rolled their eyes toward heaven and beamed a tight smile of embarrassment, and then checked their tickets before going to the pay-off windows.

But he knew better than that. To be lucky was not simply to have things go your way, but to feel that they would, to know in some mellow chamber deep in your breast that you would fill the straight or would win the photo finish. The event itself merely confirmed this welling euphoria. To be lucky was to know that you were one of the favored, like Jacob in the *Old Testament*, that the dialect of your mind was the dialect nature was speaking, that your instincts were reflexes in sync with the universe.

Or so he imagined, because he knew all this only by negation, by his not having experienced it. What he really knew was what it meant not to feel lucky, to feel that you were not one of the favored, not Jacob but a younger brother to Job, less oppressed because programmed for nothing extraordinary. It was to know you would not fill the flush, to know even as you raised with a full house that your adversary had an impossible four of a kind. It was to feel that you knew the language but not the dialect, that your instincts would betray you, that the little voice saying "Bet it all" was lying, that somewhere someone was laughing.

His life as the gambler-he-wasn't was a marathon wrestling match with this evil genius. He fought it with the patience and discipline of a monk as well as the shrewdness and caution of a banker. And he succeeded, or seemed to, if hovering near even could be called succeeding. In the long run, over twenty-five years of poker twice a week, the track at least once a week, an occasional game of craps, and an even less occasional trip to Las Vegas, this was his achievement: to have hovered near even—or, to put a fine point on it, a little below even. But what more should he want? He had the pleasure of the play at very little cost. He endured where many high rollers went the way of shame and broken lives. He had the respect of his fellow-players as an intelligent, if cautious, player. What more indeed?

If anyone had ever asked him, as no one ever did, the answer was simple: he wanted to be lucky, to feel blessed. In a phrase, he wanted to win big occasionally. After years of persuading himself that hovering near even was something to take pride in, he gradually became uncomfortable with it, as with an old sweater vaguely heavy with odors of forgotten meals and old sweat. To win ten dollars in games where real winners won two or even three hundred, to lose ten dollars when others were cashing trifecta tickets for six or seven hundred. To take pleasure in such crumbs was worse than the recklessness that led to Gamblers Anonymous. It was the story of his life, he realized one day at the races as he was simultaneously losing an exacta that would have paid him a hundred dollars and winning a straight bet that could cover his losses. He had never married, never had any children, while virtually everyone he played cards with sat at the end of soap-opera family sagas. He had a good job at the department store. His parents had left him the one-family bungalow he lived in, for the most part alone, in the neighborhood he had grown up in. He had women friends, now and then, divorcees and bachelorettes initially excited by the tracks and the treks to Las Vegas, but ultimately bored by his workmanlike fidelity to cards and to horses. And so it was. The action that had so long quickened him began to seem like the action of wheels spinning, mocking him and very slowly settling.

He was forty years old, on the ridge, he said to himself the morning of his bi-annual checkup, as he suddenly realized something disquieting had shown up in his blood test. The doctor, an athletic figure with a polished bald head and heavy glasses, counselled optimism. The disease, if he had it, was a rare blood condition that, in very plain terms, scrambled the roles of the blood's components. It came in three varieties: Type A, which was quickly fatal but extremely rare; Type B, which was slow and indecisive and a bit less rare; and Type C, which was curable by a lengthy series of injections, by far and away the most common of the three. In other words, the odds were very good, though a more sophisticated analysis would be required to determine which of the three types he had, that is if he had any at all. "But not to despair," the doctor smiled. He personally had never seen a Type A, and he had seen only one Type B in thirty years of practice, while he had seen and heard of a dozen Type Cs. "You're a gambling man, if my memory serves me. Consider the odds."

But the doctor's jauntiness didn't help. He knew the feelings he was experiencing only too well: the prickling sensation under his collar, the shallowness of his breathing, the sagging pull deep in his bowels, and most of all the unjust sense of unworthiness. The gears of the universe were meshing, the planets were spinning in fixed orbits making mystical music, seeds were blowing and falling and taking root; but not for him. He left the doctor's office and walked around the block three times before getting into his car; he called to beg off the poker game that evening (a first!) and then watched family sitcoms and wondered seriously if there were any good reasons to go on living. He went to the races on Saturday and began with two exactas which put him $250 ahead only to make a series of uncharacteristic large bets and lose it all. But he didn't mind the loss so much as that once again he ended near even. It was all too much: he must break this rondo of simple figures always returning to an unsatisfying C-major chord. He must defy whatever it was in his makeup that constrained him to cautious survival and jump the rails to another scenario.

The following week was the busiest of the year for his office: students were registering at the University and flocking to the store to buy odds and ends for their apartments and rooms. To relieve the drag that felt like a bag of sand suspended from his heart, he tried to lose himself in his accounts, in the staggeringly numerous small sales, the metamorphic inventories, the mountains of slips and computer printouts leading at the end of each day to unusually large bank deposits and daily consultations with the buyers.

It was toward the end of one such day, Thursday to be precise, as he sat at his desk before the open safe to his right, that the large stacks of small bills to be deposited first thing the following morning caught his eye as might a familiar woman-friend who has suddenly appeared without her clothes. These stacks of banded greenbacks were suddenly the way to change his life. Not all of them, he hastened to assure himself, just enough of them to make him a high roller; they were not intended to make him wealthy, but to break the pattern of running in small circles. He tapped at his calculator, one eye on the keys, the other on the bills, like junior officers awaiting his orders. What did it matter? He had already branded Type A on the inside of his forehead—wasn't it, after all, his blood type too? Anything to drive out this strangling sense that everything was fixed, sealed in tedious chains of genes in some perverse hook-up with the modalities of being.

He waited until the next afternoon, Friday, and then slipped four of the stacks of bills from those scheduled for deposit the following Monday morning into a shopping bag. Altogether, they came to $20,000. Not a great deal, but then this was not theft for profit. From the store he went directly to the airport where, thirty minutes later, he boarded the weekly excursion flight to Las Vegas.

He always went to Las Vegas a little as a doubting pilgrim goes to Lourdes. He shied from the tinselled architecture erupting in colored lights like bubbles tracing giddy explosions, the stage-lit halls upholstered to mute cries of glee and grief, the corny motifs in decor and costumes: Hollywood western, Bloomingdale Roman, Disneyland circus, all tricked out to define an unreal context for winning or losing. But all this was redeemed by the fact that here gambling was considered the most normal activity in the world, not only for the solemn blackjack buffs hunched in semicircles and the table-hopping crapshooters looking to attach themselves to hot hands, but for everyone. He drew an easy reassurance from the fact that the play was nonstop, even at 4:00 and 5:00 in the morning after the rooms had thinned and energy had abated to a trickle, and still later at 10:00 when the desert sun was already burning the sidewalk as he went to get a *Racing Form* for his afternoon in the horse rooms. Was being there and playing as unreal as everything seemed designed to suggest? Was waltzing around with lady luck essentially a dance with the shadow principles of our shadow lives? These notions teased his mind into tight little knots which he then pushed aside as he turned to the most bettable races at the four major racetracks.

He would not try to change his style, he had decided: he would not start playing horses because of their names or numbers, but would continue to handicap with the deliberation he had cultivated over many years. But he would bet more, and he would try for some long-odds exactas and trifectas. And it started well. After some initial losses, he won a two hundred dollar exacta at Arlington Park that netted him $4,500 and two straight win bets that brought him two thousand. By three o'clock that afternoon he was nearly eight thousand to the good and giddy from the thinner air. Perhaps now, he mused as he took a break for coffee and a danish in an effort to sustain his poise, he could at last think of five-dollar chips in the gaming rooms as nickels and twenty-five dollar chips as quarters. He patted the wad of new bills in his trouser pocket, pushing off the thought that if he went home now and returned the money he would still be a big winner, as he had never been before. But he couldn't do it: it would be like going home while your date is slipping into something comfortable.

Back in the auditorium with its silent handicappers and television monitors flashing odds and projecting races, he did less well in the next hour, losing three straight, then winning a bet but narrowly losing an exacta, then narrowly losing a cluster of bets keyed on a horse that was flying in the stretch but just failed to get up in the final strides. His heart thundered and something in his brain locked in neutral as he watched the rerun twice, each time swelling hopefully as his horse rushed at the leader and then unaccountably hung back, a lip from victory. He went to the bar for a drink.

This was different. Gambling had always drawn him to musings about destiny, even as one side of his mind smiled at the word. How did he stand with the universe? Good God, was he actually asking so ridiculous a question? And was it really losing a photo finish that drove him to it, or was it a deeper concern about a blood analysis that probably even now stood completed in some pathology lab?

The bar was almost deserted except for three men hunched in a group, talking in whispers, probably discussing how they stood with the universe, and a solitary woman, pretty, in her thirties, now and then looking his way. That was another thing: gambling was something, by preference, you did alone. He didn't want the distraction of another destiny entangled in his, or even fluttering quietly near him as he contemplated his own. He wanted to talk only to himself, before and after the event, and especially after. No, the three men were not talking about destiny, but more likely about whom to call for a quick loan. And the solitary woman was not looking for company; she was thinking about that last race at Belmont and the cosmic drama that had led her through it. He finished his drink, decided to let the horses finish the day without him, and went to his room to get ready for the casino.

He usually avoided roulette because it was so completely a game of chance, even though at the same time he recognized that its odds were much more favorable to the player than racing odds. Yet this first evening, still five thousand ahead, he decided to test the waters at the wheel before venturing further. Why not? A series of bets to the extent of a thousand or so just to see how the signs were conspiring. He started with conservative bets of fifty on red and black and on odd and even, and then some twenty-five dollar bets on single numbers at thirty-five to one. He lost four hundred and fifty. Undaunted, in fact sensing a rising exhilaration that lady luck was about to whisper "Take me," he doubled his bets and won with a single number, three. Impulsively, he started playing variants of three: thirteen, twenty-three, thirty-three, and he won twice more, on thirty-three and again on three. Next he doubled his bets and played multiples of three: six, nine, twelve on one turn, twenty-one, twenty-four, and twenty-seven on the next, and again he won. This inspired madness continued through the next hour and a half. He was in sync with a tempo more elusive than that of car horns in the city; he was aloft, skimming the earth. When, after six straight losses, he backed off to carry two heavy bags of chips to the cashier's windows, he was in round numbers thirty-two thousand ahead.

It had worked. He had now only to be sensible, to bet defensively, to deploy his skills, to protect his hoard and perhaps enlarge it, to wait for the rising exultation. Avoiding roulette had been a mistake: it had taken its ostensible randomness to dislodge him from pedestrian sanity and track his special wave length. He would be patient now and stay with the near even-money bets of red and black and odd and even until he felt the music return. And there was music; once again the table quivered with it. But now it was in a minor key as background to two hours of a perverse series of wrong choices. When he bet black, it came up red; when he bet odd, it came up even; when he bet red ten straight times, black came up nine of the ten times. When he lost patience and went back to single numbers, he lost continuously. It was uncanny, more sensational and dazzling, even, than his early winning streak. He looked on in numbed fascination, steadily increasing his bets, daring the universe to keep it up, as probability, as he understood it, dissolved into a clicking laughter, like dried bones on dried bones, or skulls in chorus. A few moments before he left the table, he noticed the thirtyish woman from the bar across the way, looking at him, smiling softly. Her arms were bare, beautifully rounded and, he could see, slightly freckled. Nine thousand down, he strode out of the room and through another on his way to the bar. As he passed among rows of slot machines, he looked at his change and, finding a quarter, played the nearest machine at hand. The losing combination had not yet registered when a woman with silver and copper hair, enormous jewelled glasses, and a necklace of large animal teeth pounced on him, assailing him for playing her machine while she was fetching quarters, berating him for his want of slot-machine decorum.

"But I've lost," he replied.

"That doesn't matter," she growled. She was a harpy, one of those fateful women from literature and legend who feed on the guilty. Her voice creaked above the machines, following him into the bar and the solitude of his disheveled thoughts.

Nine thousand behind. For the first time he felt like a thief. He could raise a couple thousand; he had that much in his savings account. Maybe he could borrow another five hundred quickly. But that still left him six thousand shy. He could taste the disgrace and the messy end of his job. Maybe he'd get probation and community service, and a little job in a supermarket. After all, it was his first offense. And what did it all matter anyway if next week he got the sentence of a Type A? With his luck, he thought, he probably *wouldn't* get a Type A.

He slid onto a bar stool and called for a bottle of beer. The room was large, extending beyond the bar to tables at a lower level and then a small stage at the far end where a large black woman was singing show tunes. Figures moved in and out and around the tables and bar, and the talk was brisk and lively. The evening was still young: the early shows had ended, the late ones had yet to begin, and fortunes were still to be made or lost. A large form to his left moved away from the bar to reveal the thirtyish woman with the beautiful arms on the stool beyond; as he looked and recalled her, she looked at him and smiled. A quick scenario unrolled in his mind. She's here with her husband, and she's waiting for him to finish. She doesn't gamble, but he does and he always loses while she drifts from the shows to barrooms to game rooms, where she watches until it's all over. Then they go home. She's bored and maybe a little angry, and really rather pretty in a soft and young but matronly way. Then his mind snagged. He was on the point of speaking to her, puzzled that all at once he was drawn to what he knew would be the impurity of that. There'd be too many lies to tell.

Roulette had been his mistake, a game of sheer chance that put you beyond all help of intelligence and experience. It was a lesson he had learned as a teenager, and he had forgotten it. Now he had learned it again, when it was too late, useless to him—always the way. He sat for a long time, calling for a second drink, avoiding the eyes of the woman with the round arms until she went off with a quick step. Slowly he began to feel better. As the singer banged through the second chorus of "Everything's Coming Up Roses," he reminded himself that he had not lost everything: he still had eleven thousand, he still had sixteen hours before his flight back, and he still had his considerable ability at play. In a rush it occurred to him that what he had really lost in the roulette debacle was his courage. And he knew as a second, elementary lesson that, if he was going to gamble at all, even cautiously, he could never do so without courage. To gamble without courage is like trying to eat without appetite; you can do it, but never satisfactorily. Maybe the luck of the high flyers was not for him; maybe thinking it could be or should be or might be was his mistake. Maybe believing that there were mistakes in all this, hence right and wrong choices in some wider scheme, was his error. Who said he should think this way, after all? Where was it written? He left the bar and the casino to take a taxi to the center of town where he knew he could find public poker games. He played through the rest of the night, losing at first, then winning for a period of two hours, then holding even. At about the time the players at his table began to drop out for breakfast, he had a series of hefty winning hands which took him back over the twenty thousand mark. The remaining players agreed to play one more hand.

It was a game of five-card stud, and in the first three cards he had three kings. So he bet heavily, and all the others remained in. By the fourth card two of the other four had what looked like two pair or at best three of a kind lower than kings. Another player had at least a pair, and still another could have had a small pair or could have been looking for a small straight. Again five players stayed, and the betting and raising was brisk, with the biggest bet his own. The final cards appeared to help nobody. The probable pairs or lower three of a kinds stood unchanged, and the possible straight still looked possible, though that would mean that the player had in the face of many raises drawn to an inside straight. He looked again. No, everything indicated that he had the winner. The only unknown was the sandy-haired cowboy who may have drawn to an inside straight. But why would he, in the face of such odds? At such a cost? So he raised. Two dropped out and the cowboy raised in turn. He raised again. Another dropped out, and the cowboy raised yet again. He called, and the cowboy showed him the small straight.

On an icy, snowblown Sunday afternoon many years before, his father was taking him to visit his grandmother across the city. His mother was somewhere else, probably sitting with a sick relative, so the two of them trudged through the unplowed street to the streetcar line at the end and waited. There had been a blizzard the night before and snow had drifted against the freight cars along the railroad tracks across from the streetcar stop. They waited alone for a half hour, and from time to time his father rubbed his hands and then his arms and back to warm him up, cursing their luck. Then they waited another twenty minutes. By then his feet and hands were so cold he began to cry. At last a streetcar came humming down the track from the opposite direction, and just behind that a second, and behind that a third. They would go six blocks further, where they would turn around to start the transit back across the city.

They stood looking down the track for the first streetcar to reappear, cheered that at last their desolate wait was over. And finally it did roar into view, rocking down the track, clickety-clacking on the hard steel rails, and they moved into the street where it would stop and they would climb into its heat. But it did not stop; it did not even slow down. He saw the motorman gesture to something behind him and speed on while his father cursed him and shook his fist and stamped around mumbling to himself and at last ran to a pile of construction debris and kicked at the frozen heap until he dislodged two stones the size of small balls. These he palmed, one in each hand behind his back, and he advanced again with the boy to await the second car already singing on the rails some three blocks away.

The boy knew what was coming, and he backed off several steps in disbelief. His father? His huge, warm, soft-spoken father, who never so much as spanked him? Who never raised his voice to anyone?

The streetcar was getting closer and it wasn't slowing down; and this second motorman, too, was gesturing to something behind him. But his father was ready, and as quickly as the streetcar drew near and they could see the blank expression of the motorman looking not at them but at the empty street in front of him he jerked his hands into view and shook the fisted stones at the face like wax above the throttle of the streetcar. And as the streetcar screeched past, he threw the first stone to hit the side of the car with a heavy thud and then the second to break a rear window. His father never left off cursing, and when the third streetcar slowed to a stop and let them on, he berated the third motorman as if he was the one who had passed them by, and the motorman didn't say a word.

He recalled that scene, he didn't know exactly why, as the taxi took him back to his hotel. There had been bad luck in it, yes, but there had been more, and his father's rage lashed at all of it, the luck and the non-luck. Or maybe it was the rage itself that meant something to him, the sense of outrage that there should be luck and whim and accident to defy all human understanding. He didn't grasp it all. But he did know he was comforted by the memory of his father then, furious on the frigid streetcorner, insisting on his rights and his little boy's on a snowblown, cold afternoon.

Anthony Caputi

It was already light when he settled into bed, replaying for the last few times the final game of stud. Of course the sandy-haired cowboy would lose it all, and probably quickly. Drawing to inside straights will catch up with you as surely as death and taxes. But last night the cowboy had been lucky. He had burst through a barrier that leaves you feeling ten feet tall and beautiful. The accountant set the alarm for noon: that would give him four more hours of play before his plane left.

The final four hours brought no surprises. He won a little, then lost a little, and at last left the casino still three thousand down. The next morning he went to the office at the usual time, removed the further receipts from the safe, and went to the bank. There he made up the deficit by withdrawing the two thousand five hundred in his account and arranging for a quick short-term loan of five hundred. By 10:30 he was back in his office and everything was normal. Luck? Perhaps. But he knew that his savings and his reputation had been crucial in closing the last gap.

That afternoon he went to his doctor to be told that he was neither Type A nor Type C, but Type B, more inconclusive than the other two, more ambiguous, neither a sentence of imminent death nor an absolute not guilty. He would die, like everyone else, but with care he might hold it off for a very long time, perhaps even live out his normal span. The doctor was very hopeful. In any event, it was the best he could hope for: he could stay close to even, as close as intelligence and discipline would allow. What more did he want? As he circled the block before getting into his car, he realized that that was the puzzle. What more indeed? What more, after all, could he know? He was a Type B. Today was Monday. He'd finish the day, have supper at the Red Lobster, watch *Monday Night Baseball*, and go to bed. Over the weekend he had lost some money, and tomorrow would be Tuesday. Poker! Now that his savings were gone he'd have to be careful. But then what else was new?

Anthony Caputi has published the novels *Loving Evie* and *Storms and Son*.

THE LAST GREAT FLOOD / *Bruce Bond*

We live on the flood plain where the waterfowl are
    plentiful
and news is mostly minor: two deaths,
a marriage. People here know disaster

comes every twenty-some years
down the old route of logs and immigrants.
It watermarks the restaurant walls, chalked high

like a boast, hangs in photographs
of ripped silos, Christ Cathedral humbled
to a single story. We are slow to forget

the aquarium of its sanctuary:
how the graves washed open upstream,
the cow that caught the radio tower

and would not tear away. It testifies
to the beauty here, to the long braid
of parenthood and poverty that make it hard

to leave. For the river carries little
now in the way of logs and profit.
Even as the airplane factory dragged

its bad legs to Jersey for scrap,
we stayed on by the stream of burials
and marriage, faith and the river that is its cure.

ACOUSTIC SHADOWS / *Bruce Bond*

From only a few miles away, a battle sometimes made
no sound, despite the flash and smoke of cannon and
the fact that more distant observers could hear it clearly.

As Lee pushed North and the dead flew
out of the fields in thick flocks
over Pennsylvania, the first, strange reports
went up over the wire:

from the medical tents on Wilson's Hill,
people could see the cannons
driving their nails of light
into the boarded house of the Union

and hear none of it. Who would have
believed things would go this far,
this long, the indestructible world
their intimate stranger?

For the Union soldier bound up
in what he watched, high in the near
silence, history was out there
beating its wings against the glass.

He would not move for the sight of it
and clung to his bowl of boiled coffee, watching.
All night, men returned through the dark grove,
their hands trembling like paper.

The wounded lay out on blankets in rows,
sleepless under the clear sky,
and the nails of remembered light
pinned them to their bodies.

LEGACY / *Bruce Bond*

The record needle lays down its thread
    of ruin, and the pianist dips
his hands into the crackling
    of small fires. They are old:
        his record, these hands.

If you listen close, you hear
    the pianist humming as he plays,
        especially over the slurred passages,
unable to resist: the reserved portion
    of himself stepping into the body
        of sound. He walks cautiously
into the minor movement, its slow
    recovery, turning the bare,
        remembered fragments. The hands
of the dead are his hands.
    They descend; he descends.
        They move apart, and he pauses
on the steps to feel their time
    move out from his skin and wait there.

In my dream about Beethoven,
he does not appear. The silence
    in our yard rises into two
        church doors: posed at the parish
of another century. In my dream
    about Beethoven, my father
        is driving me faster into the black
woods of D-flat. It is raining there,
    in the future where the dead wait,
        where birds are deaf to one another
and sing loud on the hardened branch:

I love the story of Beethoven's
    Ninth, how he waited
with his back to the applause,
    hearing nothing of the instant

where art ends, life begins.
We all imagined it moved him
   to turn and see the shapes of joy
   step out of his silent body:
in the future where my father lives,
   I am fitted with cold hands
   of the dead. They are what we blow
into like dice, remove
   at our bedsides to touch
   our lovers without fear. Take these
as they fall back onto their
   separate sides of the bed
   into dreams of Beethoven;
they do not hear where the record ends:
   how the needle glides into the deaf
   wood, the closing of the groove.

CHINATOWN / *Bruce Bond*

It's hot July, the year of the monkey,
and the paper lanterns hang out their hopes

for the furlough of a north wind.
People rise from the subway stairs

and fan out, skirting past the floating
crap-game, window-gates, the smell

of tangerines and marijuana.
A man steps under the brash marquee

crackling as it scrawls its one promise
always upward away from the street—

and off, then up again, a pink highball
balancing briefly on the spike heel of light.

A girl walks a cat on a string.

Inside the stripper reaches through her legs
to stroke the remaining blue scarf,

to pull it aside like a doll-house curtain:
the future is always two places;

as the broad light of fortune sets
in one, it rises in the other.

A boy blows into his dice.

Between the black booths that flirt
with never being there, the stripper

searches for the occasional
enthusiast and slides her looks

like a warm towel around him and away.
She folds her dollars carefully

into her belt, as though they too
were flesh. A man offers up

a slow stream of them, singles
in a gradual strip-tease

of his own, his money going
where he won't, a kiss

blown through the vines of smoke,
a madrigal of good rain that floats

to the north and cannot fall.

BOOK OF THE LIVING / *Bruce Bond*

If it's true, how the flesh slouches
over the tablet of itself, writing
histories of unspoken things—bad grief,
bad rage, our inconsiderate ways—
what I know as myself shuffles
the pages in its dishevelled file,
sleepless for some certainty
I cannot love. My body is an old book.
It writes itself in the poor
interior light: a wild hand:
the sources of its story trailing off
in the archives of other bodies.
Irrepressible: this love
and fear for how the body opens.
Nights I pour over tireless revisions:
the red world under its lamp,
a needy chronicle of one love's body,
the partial dream of a man with a woman's face
tattooed on his chest, her head
rimmed in a scar of flowers, deathless.

My waking is the middle of his story,
and there are tender places
in my wife's flesh where I imagine
her great sadness. Her hands gather
beneath her chest. They cannot know
what leaves or enters through these places.
She turns away, groans.
This too is how the body opens—
like an obscure and beautiful book.
It's just another miracle of desire
that leaves us missing what we never possessed.
I get up so as not to wake her
and cautiously walk through our dark
house, the narrative of rooms,
a leaky radio talking in its sleep.

My father imagines his sleeping body
opening under the surgeon's hands.
What it wouldn't do to survive
itself, to outlive the book, his own
story ashed into the vital fever.
As his ribs make their gradual way
to the surface: his lungs brandish
their shield, afraid for his diminishing
freedoms: how he can sit up in bed,
spark a match with his thumbnail,
cough into his morning cigarette.
How small he's grown, his body bent
like a clerk's under the one light.
When he doubles over, turning away
the flushed coal of his face,
the pen quickens over his heart
monitor, repeating the sweet word;
the measured passage of his flesh,
illegible, open.

Bruce Bond's collections of poetry include *The Ivory Hours, Independence Days,* and *The Anteroom of Paradise.*

LETTER FROM THE HORSE LATITUDES
/ C.W. Smith

D AD, YOUR VISIT and our agonized parting have stirred up things I'd long since hoped were still for good. Your every gesture spoke a need to ask how I came to be who and where I am.

Yet I can remember you as a fugitive. Garner State Park, Texas. We heard on the car radio the police were after you. I was eleven, thrilled to be in the company of a criminal. You who obey all laws great and small, you were deaf to the voice of Authority, fleeing the scene while Mother urged you to turn yourself in. You were (are) a lean man gnawed with American worry, quenching the fire in your gut with buttermilk and Bach, a virtuoso on your major talent—joking your way clear of painful situations.

"Calling all cars!" you boomed.

I laughed uproariously, delighted. "Who was that masked man?" My flattopped head was stuffed with what we left behind; some of those images lingered there for these many years, counting up to this afternoon.

No doubt a first for you, being pursued by the police. I recall when you became Scoutmaster for Troop #108, which met in the basement of the First Methodist church on Tuesday nights. We were uneasy about the change; to meetings your predecessor had worn the suit he sold life insurance in, but you donned, of all things, a Scoutmaster's uniform, that crap-brown adult version of our own, complete with hat and kerchief. You didn't relate to us very well. I was tormented that you were much too earnest, when I knew you privately to be a joker. Your religious air was deadly, deadly to our spirits. You never cursed, though this was consistent with your behavior at home. Your predecessor ribbed us about the lines in the Manual which counseled us to sleep with our hands above the covers, not to lie abed in the mornings, and to take cold showers when we felt "restless." He taught us the expression "loping your mule." We liked him; he knew who we were.

But you, you seemed oblivious to this side of our nature. At camp you strolled about at night leaving fruity wisps of pipe tobacco hanging in the air as you oversaw everything with the myopia we have in common, the least of many flaws that bind us. What's going on in the tents of the Phantom Buffalo Patrol is better left unacknowledged. Tonight, we "Phantom Butt-holes," as we're known, are trying to live down our name in a marathon farting contest. After lights are out and you've retired, we scoot out in the dark to other tents, stumbling onto cornhole orgies, barging in where the victor of a circle-jerk is sweeping up his winnings. The Explorers smoke Luckies on the sly, talk about getting your finger in it, heady stuff to we Phantom Butt-holes. Behind the law, life goes on. A dangerous freedom crackles in the air, but you are asleep already.

It's not likely you've forgotten how proud I did you on the rifle range, but let me tell you why: for one, I take instruction exceedingly well; for another, what I saw in the targets helped. The scoutmasters gathered just behind me on the firing line talked about Korea, where things hadn't gone well since "Frozen Chosin." I was paying close attention, having filled two scrapbooks with AP Wirephotos and traced undulations of the battlelines on a map. Although I was only twelve, I'd heard Mother wish that the war would be over before I got older. She had good reason to fear: my secret ambition was to be the next Audie Murphy. Gradually, the conversation turned on the axis of collective guilt, and you all began trading credentials from the Big One. Last in line, you chuckled and told these bombardiers and dogfaces about your draft-exempt job in the oil fields, how with the "Home Guard" you went to the beaches to drill by tossing beer cans filled with sand into the surf, and the closest your unit came to danger was when a German sub was alleged to have surfaced five miles out in the Gulf from Galveston. You made no pretense that you would have preferred the thick of things—no, you made a joke of yourself, and even though they accepted you that way, I shut my eyes and concentrated on my target. The bull's-eye was a yellow head with slanting eyes. I sent many a round cracking up its nostrils and at the end of the day I won a plaque. My best shooting was from the sitting position, where I was calm, rock-steady in my aim because the sling was wrapped around my left forearm. The tautness of it was sensual, strangely comfortable, and familiar. This was the arm I wrapped my security blanket about as a child.

The armies I've belonged to! I'm thinking now of the rag-taggle corps we ten-year-olds of the neighborhood formed on Saturdays and in the summers. We made "longjohn" pistols out of one-byfours with clothespins nailed to their handles—these fired loops of rubber cut from an inner tube and at close range left a satisfactory welt on a victim's arm or cheek; we made derringers out of clothespins that shot matchheads that burst into flame in mid-flight. Lucky souls got BB guns for Christmas; Ron McLaughlin had the fullest blessings fortune could bestow upon one so young—a Crossman pellet rifle. Twenty-five pumps and it sent a projectile clean through a tin can.

Saturday mornings we wheeled our bikes down to the Army Surplus store where the Big One's debris lay in musty heaps for our inspection: helmet liners, entrenching tools, canteens and covers, cartridge belts, packs, messkits, now and then something truly exotic like the plexiglass waistgunner's bubble we all chipped in to buy and dragged home behind our bikes to place over a foxhole dug in the pasture, instantly putting us right over Hamburg with the Jerries at 12 o'clock high! WWII canteens were made from a heavier metal than the later models, and mine had an elongated crease in its flank made, I was sure, by a grazing bullet. I would sit in my foxhole, draw out the canteen, take a swig of Kool Aid, and think: *This belonged to a guy who got shot at! I wonder if he got killed?*

We acted out situations we'd seen in the movies. We were informal scholars of a genre rich in subclasses: Marines Establish a Beachhead, Army Air Corps Raids German Ball-Bearing Plant, Dogfaces Confront Panzer Tanks, Crippled Sub Hides from Jap Destroyer, Aircraft Carrier Attacked by Kamikazis. No aspect of the Big One went untouched by Hollywood, and we saw almost every movie that came to town. By age eleven or twelve, my knowledge of military lore—ranks, chains of command, nomenclature for aircraft, ships, armored vehicles, shoulder weapons, geography—far outstripped my knowledge of any other subject. I built balsa replicas of the P-51 Corsair, the Grumman Hellcat, the B-26 Liberator, the B-17 and B-36 bombers, light and heavy cruisers, destroyers, carriers, the Patton and Sherman tanks. My bedroom sky was alive with planes twirling in perpetual dogfights on the ends of their strings. Battles waged on my dresser top between opposing forces of green plastic soldiers. I read "war funny books." I drew elaborate battle scenes, taking care to sketch in the tracers—even then I knew that every fifth round fired by a .30 or .50 caliber machine gun lit up to show you where you were firing.

Oh yes, and instructions in hand-to-hand combat. On our patio you are lying in the hammock President/General Eisenhower told you to buy to save us from a recession. Time for my boxing lesson. I've primed myself by looking at your Golden Gloves medals under glass in your bedroom. A lightweight but fast. The gloves were a birthday present; they are huge, ruddy beehives on the ends of my arms, but on your knots of fist they are taut as sausage skins. Up from the hammock, you discuss stances, hovering over me to guide my arms and legs. There's jabs and hooks and uppercuts and haymakers and not getting hit in the breadbasket; there's not telegraphing your punches, keeping your chin tucked into your shoulder, presenting only a thin, protected profile to your opponent, feinting and following through, and, of course, not hitting below the belt or in the clinches. We spar; you bloody my nose by intentional accident. But it's all right—two days later I'm able to pass it on: my playmate from across the street refuses to return to me the tack hammer that is his, and so we go at it in the street, me with my dukes in the proper place, flailing away joyously and connecting right and left. His mother screams from her stoop for us to stop fighting. Behind me, I heard you yell, "Aw, let 'em scrap!" I redouble my efforts until he runs home bawling and bleeding about his nose and mouth. I saunter up our walk, flipping the hammer from handle to head in my palm. You smile. (In high school I learned refinements you may not know, such as carrying a roll of dimes in my fist, or adding "brass knucks" which we secretly turned out in Metal Shop.)

I knew that war was a very important, dramatic activity in which men were expected to perform brave deeds for which they were rewarded by medals whose titles and appearances I knew, as well as the names of a good many of their winners and the circumstances under which they'd been won. And, of course, a hero's unofficial reward was the good memory of those whose lives had been saved—the funny little guy from Brooklyn dives onto the grenade at the last second and saves his platoon, and they remember him as a hero. When I rushed up out of my foxhole to charge the machine gun nest against suicidal odds, going "dow-dow-dow" and diving behind a clump of buffalo grass to roll into a firing position, a great tingling shot up and down my spine and made me break out in a sweat at the nape of my neck, and when I hurled my "grenade" (a clump of West Texas sandstone), ducked to wait for the blast, then charged, spraying the survivors with hot lead, I knew this was how I would've acted had I been to fight the Big One, and that soaring thrill of facing danger and being proved a man was the play's reward.

But not, though, its strategic purpose: that lore we nursed on so avidly was as purposeful as it was entertaining—I passed into puberty used to the idea of killing and dreaming I was ready to get my share.

Korea passed. The ever-present Cold War kept on heating up. Religion confused me. The killing I had played at during elementary school had given me a simple thrill. After religion, killing became more urgent, more important, more a matter of duty. Killing was expressly forbidden by my Christian religion, but now it also seemed that I would be required to kill because of it: I believed in God, but the Russians didn't. Or, rather, the leaders of the Russians didn't, but the people did and weren't allowed to say so. For this reason, I might have to kill them whether it was fun or not, like eating oatmeal, though the possibility of having to do it personally was becoming remote because of our H-bomb, which, as everyone was fond of saying, would make the ones we dropped on Japan "look like a firecracker!"

You were (are) a religious man. You took me to church, and my own creeping tendrils reached skyward for that rarefied air of religious mystery; my head swam with hymns, prayers, chants and stories (man of battles), and so in time I was washed in the blood, of the Lamb. Inevitably, the two concepts of God and Country tied into one knot. Once under the bleachers at our junior high school, during lunch hour, prompted by I have no idea what national catastrophe, I prayed for God to give America guidance. Although the word was not present in my vocabulary, the notion lurked at the dark perimeter of the prayer—Fatherland. This was God the Father's land. Other property was condemned.

Across the nation fallout shelters were hastily excavated in back yards and Civil Defense became an issue. Wardens were appointed, volunteers lined up to post signs and pack emergency supplies. Weapons were swept from den walls and carried to shelters to be used not on the Russians, who would probably not appear in person, anyway, but on neighbors who tried to take refuge in shelters not their own. A great upsurge of admiration arose to praise the proverbial ant and to disparage the grasshopper. The Civil Air Patrol initiated a plane-spotting procedure; we studied silhouettes to identify the Migs and the TUs. A couple of hours a week on the top of a windblown observation tower constructed at the edge of the city park, a good three hundred miles from the Gulf of Mexico, I scanned the sky with binoculars for that stray Russian plane which had crept under our radar screens.

I suppose you assumed all was well when I joined ROTC. We marched in front of the high school carrying our mock M-1s, each of us dying for the chance to call cadence when we rounded the corner near where the girls played softball. The National Guard Armory had real M-1s, and once every two weeks we held classes there to learn disassembly and care of the weapon. Order of arms. By my senior year I was a member of the rifle squad; we came onto the field at half-time in our white helmet liners and dress gloves to do flashy Queen Anne salutes. The crowds roaring approval and a fever shimmering in the air always told me we were primed and fit as cannon fodder; that must have been reassuring in those times.

Vietnam. You didn't know, Dad, how hard I tried to stall off my graduation as a history major. But the growing war became a labyrinth of problems in ethics, morality and national purpose that time would not allow me to sort out before the draft board came calling. Many friends joined the Peace Corps or were active in the anti-war movement. I took the path of least resistance, stayed true to my training, and joined the War Corps. But instead of letting myself be inducted into the Army, I let an old chimera loom up to play me for a fool. If I had to go, I was determined to be a grunt, to get to the front, and return to document the horrors of war—each condition part of the sentimental and anachronistic baggage I'd carted around from my matinee days.

Life with the USMC at San Diego was similar to life with the ROTC and the BSA with a dash of hate and death added, like a picante sauce. You might recall I wrote to you to make the standard recruit's complaints about the petty acts of discipline—scrubbing the concrete floor of our Quonset hut with toothbrushes in the middle of the night, duck-walking the five hundred yards to the mess hall—which our drill instructors inflicted upon us with the zeal of fraternity boys initiating their pledges, and my complaints could have been characterized as the perfunctory grievances of the pledge who fully expects to take his hardwon place on the permanent roll. The marching, the regimented schedule, the Rifle (though by then the M-16 had replaced my beloved M-1), the uniforms, the orders, the inspections, the protocol—it was all familiar, all to be expected; I did well, took care never to be first or last and could have breezed right onto a plane for Nam were it not for an unexpected development.

The lectures annoyed me more and more. Lessons in Communism was taught by an aging Gunnery Sgt. with surely not more than a fourth-grade education who persisted in making one factual error after another when he actually stuck to the subject, and he habitually dragged up his experiences in Korea as proof of his generalizations about the nature of communism. These gooks had diabolical means of brainwashing the hordes under their whip so that they seemed hypnotized and were fanatically dedicated and loyal, but it wasn't like our kind of loyalty—it was more like being drugged or hopped up, and this sometimes made them very difficult to kill or get information from; for example, once he and three other noncoms took this gook bitch out of a village and tried to get her to tell them about enemy troop movements, but she kept claiming she didn't know anything "even when we rammed a shovel handle up her cunt."

Maybe I should have written to you about that. Several times my left hand jumped like a fish in my lap from the old classroom reflex to place an objection, but aside from my fear of openly questioning him, how could I have untangled his thoughts or have made a comment which protocol would demand be a question ending with, "Sir?" This classroom situation was like none I had ever experienced—the pupils were receivers whose only permissible comment was that they didn't fully understand.

I squirmed a lot, and that affected my equanimity, the suspended judgment that had allowed me to join. Outside camp in the streets of the nation, others of my generation—some my friends, no doubt—were organizing to head us off at the pass before we could reach the terminals, lying down in the streets and on the tracks. Our Drill Instructors' vocabularies had become enriched with newly coined epithets such as "long-haired hippie queers" and "pinko fuck-face." Coupled with more traditional curses such as "yellow bastard" and "spineless fucker," the result was frequently amusing combinations such as "yellow hippie fucker!" which, to my ear, rang like the name of an exotic eel. Emerson's famous question to Thoreau began to haunt me. Or Thoreau's answer, rather. In moments of levity, or when they wished to reward us with a compliment to our fitness, our DIs cracked jokes about how they longed to march us into a peace demonstration and let us go to work scattering yellow hippie fuckers right and left, a prospect that gnawed at me at night—I could too easily picture a street scene, my friends on one side of the barricades, myself on the other. There were two worlds—the inside and the outside—and I was safe only so long as they didn't mix.

Did I write you about the lesson in the grenade? I may have left out the most significant part. This occurred at Camp San Onofre in the dusty, barren hills outside San Diego. Early evening. The class was held in a natural amphitheater lying in a valley between two ridges; three platoons of us sat in bleachers facing the waning sunlight that streamed over the top of the ridge before us and blanketed the bleachers. Before the lecture, we were smoking—a rare treat!—our bellies plump with chow; the day was almost over, and an almost festive mood was about to descend on me; the bleachers hummed with small talk, grabass, and you might have thought we were about to see a movie. Our instructor was a portly black E-6 with a jocular manner who actually got a laugh or two from us before getting down to business. The new grenade, called the "M-4" (if memory serves me right) was, he said, a *deadly* weapon. Your old grenade (I knew it well—the old "pineapple" in those films and comics) threw out shrapnel from its cover when it burst, shrapnel of limited quantities and of a size which would kill instantly or cause a wound which would be easily repaired—the chunk of metal could be located quickly. Now, your M-4 grenade (here he smirked), your M-4 has a thick jacket of steel mesh, like layers of chicken wire, and when it explodes it embeds these small bits of wire into the meat and tissue and bloodstream where they burrow slowly through the body like parasites, killing just as well, but taking a lot longer to do it and requiring more persons to attend to the wounded while he's dying; therefore, it is a more effective weapon: it maims and debilitates, turning fatal only as the last step in a slow process.

"Beautiful, huh?" Silhouetted against the setting sun, he held up the grenade. "Now what is this?"

Rousing from our indolence: "Uh, M-4 grenade, sir!"

"What? Can't hear you!"

"M-4 Grenade, Sir!" we rumbled, louder.

"And what is it?"

Some confusion—we can't recall our lines. "Ah.,...uh...Deadly, Sir!"

"What does it DO?"

"Kills, Sir!"

"Can't hear you!"

"KILLS, SIR!"

Some tittering; he is biting back a grin, and we are grinning in return as we yell.

"All right! Once again—what does it DO?"

Screaming: "KILLLSSSSSS, SSSIRRRR!"

An echo bounded down that valley between the ridges—*illls illls illlsss irr irr irr*—and in that golden light hazy with motes, the declining sun warm against my face at the tranquil end of day, full-bellied, grinning, yelling this harrowing chant, I felt my third eye open and pull back from the scene to show me two hundred strange beasts clad in green gathered upon a strange planet to yell a mad blood-cry in unison, chortling as they did, and I wondered suddenly: are we a crime against nature or the very expression of it?

This was psyching up; our instructor was our cheerleader, and we were hollering for blood, priming ourselves to do the letting. I really didn't fear dying—I was much too young to believe I could—but I saw I was on my way to killing, inching closer every day, every lesson in the techniques and psychology of it bringing me sidled alongside it, the hate they tried so hard to instill in me working like the blinders to keep the horse from leaping out of its traces.

I'd presumed the men who led me would be worthy of being followed, would set an example for me to measure up to. But with one exception (Sgt. Lacey), the DIs were corrupt, venial men, coming around on payday to collect for "relief funds" which we knew were nonexistent except as euphemisms for their own welfare; they enjoyed their cruelty; they dealt out an arbitrary justice, following the rules when it was to their advantage, taking Kafkaesque interpretations of them when it wasn't; they were paranoid; they sought excuses to use their hands and feet on us. I had expected them to be hard to please (part of the glamour of the Marines was the acclaimed "toughness") but found them neurotically picayunish; I expected sternness and saw only rigid aggression. Above all, I'd expected them to be self-disciplined, self-denying. But they hardly, if ever, denied themselves anything they denied us. They drank all the water they wished on long, dusty hikes and hitched rides on passing Jeeps. They were unintelligent men whose liberties were spent, by their own jocular admission, beating up "queers" and abusing whores and getting blind drunk.

No man exemplified this more that Sgt. Spores. In the years since, when I've talked about him I've usually gotten an indulgent but incredulous smile from my listener because the figure of the sadistic DI is a stock character in almost any bootcamp anecdote, dozens of which I too had heard before I joined. Spores fit the stereotype so well that at first I thought he was only playing a role, but later I came to believe that his part had become fused to his personality so that he could no longer separate them: the role itself drew on some inward rage that both channelled and fueled it. The chicken-and-egg cycle of art imitating life also occurred to me. Spores had seen too many John Wayne movies, and he tried to imitate Jack Webb's role in *The DI*, itself a cliché derived from life.

Ramrod straight bearing? Hardly. Sgt. Spores was a skinny man whose terrible posture produced, in profile, the appearance of a thick snake clothed in military garb trying to stand on its tail. He had a misshapen head wide at the top and compressing inward at the temples and rounding again at the bottoms of his jaws, like the body of a guitar. Thick wet red lips pursed perpetually like a sphincter; two eyes like metal buttons, shallow and lifeless, above which lay thin brows almost albino-blonde. Holder of a black belt in karate, or so he claimed. (Jesus, I hated him. Still do. Over twenty years later now, and my teeth grind as I write this.) Other biographical details of interest include his confession that "I married me a gook and regretted it ever since" and the habit of cupping his left hand like a ball glove and chopping its palm with a karate-rigid heel of his right, except when other targets were handy, such as telephone poles and the napes of our necks. He couldn't keep his hands off us, and these sadistic caresses came to be etched on my crawling flesh with nightmarish clarity: he loved to clamp your carotid artery between his thumb and index finger; he dug his digits under your collarbone; he jabbed your Adam's apple with a hand drawn up in a claw; he'd wrench your ear like a schoolmarm; he'd knee you in the thigh and give you a Charlie-horse; he'd knee you in the balls.

Like all other DIs, Spores played favorites, and the apple of his eye was "Private Asshole," a black kid from rural East Texas who must have stood on tip-toe to meet the height requirement and eaten sourdough laced with lead to come up to weight. Private Asshole, whose real name I've forgotten, was a jittery sort, and finding himself receiving so much of Sgt. Spores' attention didn't increase his self-confidence. He was singled out in orders: "I want those rifles cleaned by 1400 hours, and that means yours, too, Private Asshole!" Or "smoking lamp's lit for one cigarette, except for you, Private Asshole." Pvt. A invariably had to run ten laps around the platoon to get his mail; his rifle never once passed inspection (nor his rack, foot locker, uniform); he always did twice our calisthenics, twice the distance we ran, and had to remain behind to stand at attention guarding our stacked rifles while we went in to chow, was then given five minutes to eat, etc.

Pvt. A had the eyes of a skittish colt, large, brown watery orbs set in a milk-blue jelly, and they flicked constantly like hyper-alert antennae. He hardly ever spoke, made no friends, received mail from a single source—his "Mama," whose letters revealed (A was made to read two aloud) that he hadn't finished high school and joined the service because he needed a job, the Marines because the Army recruiter had been out to lunch. He was the smallest of us, the quietest, probably the youngest (I doubted he was truly 18), blackest; he took this punishment from Spores with a barely muted desperation, and so with a greasy ease he came quickly to be our scapegoat, too. Insults did not rebound; punches were not returned. Hating Spores as we did, Pvt. A's role as ritual goat got us off his hook, even helped explain why Spores hated us: if only we could rid ourselves of A, then maybe Spores would get off our backs, we secretly thought. We had noticed (thanks to Spores's pointing it out) that A had two lefts of everything: hands, toes, fingers, thumbs—he always left-shoulder-armed to our right, left-faced alone, and persisted in lagging two out-of-steps behind his rank, marking us as raw boots when we longed to look like vets as we were marched by the Receiving barracks, our own heels clomping out our cadence. And Spores would explain our collective punishment in terms of one man's crime: "No letter-writing tonight, maggots! You can thank Pvt. Asshole for that!"

By the time we reached the point in our training when we were to go to the rifle range, our platoon had shed its "ten-percenters," that statistical grouping of physical and psychological washouts—one broke a leg, one confessed to being homosexual, one had an outbreak of rheumatic fever, and one had recurring nightmares that woke us all with blood-chilling screams. "Ten-percenters" were pariahs ("ten-percenter" was as an epithet as scalding as "maggot" or "individual"), and, though Spores tried to place Private A in that category, A hung onto his place on the roster as we left for the range. Meanwhile, Spores had stressed the supreme necessity for each man to qualify with his rifle; there was no greater humiliation for a DI than to have a boot fail to qualify, nor was there a greater shame for the recruit. The Marine Corps wasn't like other branches of the service (which by implication were populated by cowards, morons, and perverts); in The Crotch even a cook learned to shoot properly and effectively. So still another pitfall yawned before our feet as the two-week stint went by and Qualifying Day came around.

Not to anyone's great surprise, Pvt. A was the only recruit in our platoon who did not qualify, due in no small part to the help

Spores gave by standing over him with one boot planted on either side of his hips as he lay on the firing line, yelling as A jerked his trigger and sent round after round spewing dirt up in the butts and getting a red flag—"Maggie's drawers"—from his target-pullers. A last riddle in a self-fulfilling prophecy had been revealed; we were free to hate him, he who disqualified in our stead.

In saner moments, I could have untangled the dynamics of the whole wretched syndrome, beginning with Spores's bigotry and ending where it did, but I wasn't altogether in my right mind, and how I've worked to come back to it is not just part but parcel of what this letter is about. Then, though, I seethed with everybody else because Pvt. A had incurred Sgt. Spores's wrath on the lot of us, and we had to run back to tent camp from the range at a port-arms doubletime. Sepulvida, running just behind A, kept kicking A's bony little ass as we huffed and panted through the hills in the dust and heat, dying for water and still three miles to a stop. We were supposed to have had a piss call before running back to camp, as we had been out on the range since just before noon without one, but Spores had denied it for obvious reasons, so many of us were suffering the maddening, paradoxical pangs of an aching bladder and a parched mouth. It's notable that Spores ran the whole way with us that afternoon, part of the syndrome being his need to feel that Pvt. A was punishing *him*, forcing him to run five miles in the heat and dust of a California summer afternoon. Therefore, Pvt. A would pay.

"I . . . said," Spores gasped when he had halted us in raggedy-assed formation outside our tents, "I wanted every one of you turds to qualify!" His chest heaved, and sweat dripped off his jawline. "And you didn't. FUCKERS!" He panted a moment, and we huffed with him. "DID I SAY YOU COULD PISS YOUR PANTS!!!" he bellowed suddenly, and in an instant was hovering over Pvt. A. "DID YOU HEAR ME GIVE YOU A PISSING ORDER!"

I cast a sidelong glance. A large dark spot was spreading over Pvt. A's trousers. He was not alone—I spotted two others. I was about to go, too.

"No, Suh!"

"YOU MAGGOT!" The cuff to A's temple almost bowled him over, then he cried the first public words he had ever uttered in his own defense. "I couldn't help it, Suh!"

Spores writhed and trembled in speechless agitation in front of him for a few seconds. He then turned and gave us all three minutes for a piss call (except for A, of course), and sixty-one of us dashed frantically for the eight toilets in the head, popping buttons as we ran and stampeding into the building, slung rifles clattering, bristling and jabbing; we pissed all over each other's boots and pants' legs then sprinted madly back into formation. A and Spores had vanished.

"At Rest, you fuckers!" Spores yelled from inside the duty tent just behind us. "Water up. Lamp's lit for one cigarette."

Gratefully, we unhusked canteens and lit up, our bladders lax as old balloons. Unlike "Parade Rest," the position of "At Rest" allowed us to pivot about upon one stationary foot, the left. We were free to talk, and with A's fate now a private matter between him and Spores, we took leisurely drags off damp, curled cigarettes and cooled down after the five-mile run. A low mumble arose as everyone tried to work high scores into conversation or rationalize low ones.

"Shit maggot!" we heard from the duty tent behind us. There were titters in the formation: who gave a rat's ass if A was going to get another cussing?

"Nigger turd!"

A few snickers chirped up in the ranks above the general mumble. Ross pivoted around to look toward the duty tent and raised an eyebrow to me.

"What'd you shoot, man?"

We heard a low keening, like a continuous whimper.

"NIGGER MAGGOT!"

An idiotic fury erupted in Spores's voice; Ross and I almost burst into laughter to hear this insane gibberish of frustration, Spores's anger having stripped him of what was an already meagre imagination. Poor A, I thought.

"One twenty-eight," I said.

I was half-expecting Spores to carry the spare handful of grammatical components to its nonsensical conclusion with "shit turd!" but instead we heard a thump and a clatter, followed by a moan. Pivoting on my left foot, I saw the side of the duty tent pop outward driven by a round projectile I feared was A's head, then the canvas side fell slack, and we heard sobbing. One side wall of the duty tent had been rolled up from the bottom for ventilation, and now we could see that A had fallen to the floor, the heel of one boot visible at the edge of the wooden deck the tent was pitched upon; the rest of the interior was dim, with vague green shapes in motion.

A curse was choked back, as though Spores had tried to shout but was strangling on his own phlegm, then I could make out a black shape in a swift arc which ended abruptly in a green form, and an "Oww! Uh!" as Spores's boot landed somewhere on A's body. Three more times, and each connection was a muffled *thut!* in the air.

A began crying, "Don't Suh! Please don't no more, Suh!"

Another flurry of blows. "Maa Maaa!" A's wailing penetrated our chatter like a siren.

"What'd ya get prone on the 500?" Ross was knocking on my arm to get my attention. He was nervous, his face flushed, squinting at me almost angrily.

"What?" I asked, confused. I kept twisting on my left foot to turn from his oddly agitated face to the duty tent where a clatter of overturning furniture told me Spores wasn't finished yet.

"I shot a forty-six," said Ross. "How about kneeling and sitting, what'd ya do?" He bobbed on his feet and spat toward the duty tent. We heard another cry of pain. "I got a forty-six!"

Looking down the ranks I saw that several others were sending quick, nervous glances behind them toward the duty tent. A few were elbowing each other, grinning and gesturing furtively. Still the crashing, the muffled knocks, the cursing and the sobbing went on—I pictured Spores picking A up by his collar and tossing him around. If we weren't At Rest, I thought, I'd go in there and . . . what? I didn't know. My left foot was rooted in place, and I kept hobbling about in a circle like an animal with one paw caught in a trap.

At last all sound ceased from the tent.

"I . . . got a forty-four," I told Ross.

After a moment, Spores appeared in the doorway to his tent, sweating and serene. "Stack your rifles, wash up and get back in formation in ten minutes for chow," he said quietly.

We never saw Pvt. Asshole again; Spores kept him in the duty tent for the rest of the afternoon and evening, and when he got a chance, Pvt. A tried to go over the hill, collapsed outside of camp, was discovered by a family of civilians and returned to Sick Bay, where he was immediately operated on for a "burst appendix," according to reports filtering back to us.

During the remaining weeks of training I was plagued by recurring cameo memories: A's bootsole resting on the floor of the duty tent, a man plunging into a river. These images were flags, a semaphore of something gone wrong, though I didn't know it, then. Marching on, I ignored them. Now Spores and the platoon could hold our heads high; the record showed every recruit had qualified; the record showed that we had shed all our "ten-percenters." Now there was no essential difference between what Spores was and what we had become.

What happened to Pvt. Asshole? Some brave soul ventured one night as we stood lighting up during the last smoking lamp of the day, encouraged by Spores's admission he was proud of us.

"Aw!" Spores spat. "That fucker couldn't even shine his shoes."

Later, we heard he would be court-martialed and given a Bad Conduct Discharge, when he healed. He had no business here. He was not one of us. (We had seen to that.) Wasn't he better off on the outside? Weren't we better off without him? Wasn't Spores happier? Weren't we more at ease?

Yes, to all accounts. There would always be that ten percent, so don't sweat it, I kept counselling myself, only to be answered by that image of A's boot, then the clip of a lean man with white skin surging into the water in his baggy boxer shorts. How these images were connected, I couldn't say.

I posed as proudly as any for the platoon's graduation picture and spent the morning strutting on the grinder before the admiring eyes of my fellow Marines' sisters and girlfriends, reliving the ancient ROTC urge for display, the glamour of it a reward for those weeks of struggle.

But the bubble burst the minute I stepped onto the plane for home. I was afraid that alone I would utter something to myself I didn't want to hear, and I longed to be back with the platoon, to be reassured that the process that had produced what I had become was a legitimate and healthy undertaking for human beings.

"Welcome home, killer!" Thus, grinning, you greeted me as I walked into the terminal, jabbing me lightly and affectionately on my shoulder. My uniform impressed you, made you proud, but my blush was not from modesty. Nor was it modesty that kept me from putting the uniform back on again once I had changed into civvies. Clothes.

I wanted to tell you something then, but I didn't know how to say it and wouldn't for several years, wouldn't, really, until our meeting this week. Two and a half decades is a long time to avoid a subject, I know. My silence even seems *historic*, somehow; it began in '64 when I became a fugitive here and kept on even after I'd been "pardoned" by Carter, and continued even after you'd relented and come to visit. If you had asked me then, eons ago during that leave, if something were bothering me, I could have only said I was carrying two pictures in my head but didn't see how they were related. You didn't ask; I didn't volunteer. Instead, I spent two weeks spinning yarns, letting legends substitute for what I really had to say, hiding behind the aura of "Marine" as you introduced me around your office. I experienced a wave of nausea on being shown the clipping from our local paper in which I appeared in my helmet, a grim tuck to my lips appropriate for one undergoing the rigors of learning to kill. Awkward moments arose when the TV showed protesting students going limp or being tear-gassed; people would try to coax a fang-baring from me, but I clammed up in silences that were read as slow-burns.

I've always been glad I took the hard way back to California; it's as if I unconsciously knew I had something to work out and my mind produced the 18-hour bus trip as a hiatus for it. Near El Paso, my fingernails were tiny particles suspended in my saliva. Germany, all those thousands silent while the ovens burned. (Oh, come on! Don't be melodramatic!) Still, why hadn't I done something? (Such as?) Such as stopping Spores from beating A. (But you couldn't, you know? You were "At Rest"; one foot belonged to you, but the other had been planted in place by the order, and you couldn't very well go into the duty tent without lifting your left foot, even if the right was free to go. Nobody else did anything, either. A's fate was inevitable; he was a ten-percenter.)

Phoenix. Images arising from the ashes of my recent past: when they coalesced, what shape would call itself by my name? I twisted and turned in my seat and butted my head against the window of the bus. My conscience didn't care that no one else had acted, and as for A's "fate," it was one thing to tell a man he isn't suited for the Corps, give him his papers and a ticket for home, and quite another to bedevil him for thirteen weeks until he cannot perform, kick him repeatedly in the ribs, stomach and back until an organ ruptures, then toss him out with a BCD. (But you couldn't move that left foot, you know—)

What, was it staked to the sand? Was I in leg irons?

Before the bus reached Barstow, I got the shakes; at 2 a.m. the desert was a refrigerated plain illuminated by a full moon's bony light. The claims my culture had made on me seemed overwhelming, and I felt I had been tooled on an assembly line. I thought when I got back I would report what Spores had done to the company's commanding officer or to my congressman. Then I worried that, back among them all, their control over my mind would be reasserted and I'd be argued out of it. That left foot was indeed staked to the sand, I saw, and that stake was in my mind. Too much of me belonged to them, too much of me was part of the mob.

I got off the bus at Barstow and stewed around inside the depot hoping to make little acts of dawdling constitute a larger choice. Sipped a Coke, trembling, then at the last minute before time to depart for L.A., I got the driver to abort my sea-bag from the belly of the bus and stood on the curb watching the vaporous spume of diesel-wash obscure its taillights as it swept on west without me.

How I remember your first visit here. "Nobody knows how things will turn out," you mused, puffing on your pipe as you broke a silence of five years. (A very noisy silence, I might add: your thoughts crossed a thousand miles of prairie to become a voice in my head. My son, the deserter.) Turning to peer at you as we strolled down the earthen path to see the new piglets and the calf, I was a little surprised to discover I'm taller and heavier than you. Your smile was bemused; your comment was inspired by the disorientation of your long plane ride and the tangible reality of my life as a part-time teacher and farmer here on the Saskatchewan plain, living in "sin" with a woman and fathering a child not my own who might as well have been dropped on my stoop by gypsies (though he's your grandson, should you choose to think so). Later, while Mother and Betsy skirmished politely in the kitchen, we sat in my study (at least, this is my memory of it), you on your second beer and I on my eighth, your eyes taking embarrassed probes at my props, my icons: posters of Uncle Sam with his middle finger waggling obscenely, of a nude woman in a provocative pose, of a giant marijuana leaf. Book covers implied that my heroes were now insane black men who brandish machine guns and Maoism; other texts whispered of drug-lunacy, rituals of hallucination and mysticism. Conspicuously absent were the sorts of texts which guided our ancestors—Confederate army officers, plantation owner, merchants, mayors, bond brokers, realtors—on their trek to prosperity and posterity: your Bibles, your Boy Scout Handbooks, the Wall Street Journal.

At last we generated a conversation based on illusory nostalgia. We batted about the lives of my high school classmates; I inquired desultorily about them, and you supplied the information, rather wistfully I might add, that for the most part they were careered, married, childrened, moving upward in institutional echelons, arguing cases, curing diseases.

"What about Ron McLaughlin?" I asked.

"He's dead," you said. You might remember there was an abrupt silence, then you blurted out: "He got killed in Vietnam." Oh Christ! A flash of anger shot out before you could check it—don't deny it!—indignation, really: now wasn't I sorry I didn't go? Or maybe for an instant you thought it was my fault he was killed because I wasn't there to help him. Didn't "support" him by believing the war was justified. But then I watched your face contort and sweep through different phases, struggling to return to neutrality: you saw at once how absurd and terrible it was to wish Ron's fate on me, and I saw how readily you would have and burst into laughter, at the absurdity of our cross purposes, at our embarrassment. I hope you didn't regret it that after a minute you began to chuckle also, despite your wish to keep a grave face out of respect to the dead.

Then we simply dropped the subject for another twenty years. You know how these things go: it's not that time makes it easier to be silent; it makes it harder to speak. Over the years I got the hints—how "happy" you were for me that I'd been "pardoned"; I know that eased your mind about what I'd done, but I didn't need to be told by an American president that it was permissible not to kill peasants on the other side of the globe, and his "pardon" only made it possible for me to come to Austin. I may, still. Meanwhile, our letters grew longer over the years, but we never touched on this.

But yesterday, I sensed we were ready. I'm grateful you brought up the business about my great-great-grandfather, Tyrone, not only because it revealed you had been parting the branches of the family tree to find some precedent to justify me, but because it led me to this business about yourself as a fugitive. Yes, I did remember that Tyrone was an officer in the military escort that marched the Cherokees from Georgia to Oklahoma on the famous "Trail of Tears," and I also recall that afterward he refused "every dime" of his pension. You wanted to be as proud of that act of conscience as you were of me in my uniform; you wanted to be proud of my reasons for "desertion," but you weren't certain you could be. Though a glimmer of mirth played in your eyes, the sadness dragged at your mouth, the skin along your jaw hung loose, and I could almost hear you think: such a fine shot! Such good grades! And an Eagle Scout!

You didn't tell the rest of the story, either because you'd forgotten it or because you didn't want to remind me that conscience-stricken as old Tyrone was, when they reached the end of that Trail of Tears he dashed right back to Georgia to stake a claim on a sizeable portion of the land he had just run the Cherokees off of, so he had more to atone for than was indicated in your tale. What his story says is that his conscience was strong enough to irritate, but not reform, him. Giving up that pension? An empty gesture.

But I felt a kinship with old Tyrone. I knew then why I'd never talked with you about my going over the hill. I secretly feared I might discover my reason wasn't as sound as I'd hoped. In those earlier years here, when you came to visit, I was playing the exile; I was an expatriate who had left America because it wanted me to kill Third World peasants in a senseless war. Now, another decade and a half later, my own history has suffered revisionism; I came to Canada in a effort to dignify two successive failures: the failure to help poor Pvt. A and the subsequent failure to return to the ranks and right the wrong done him. Refusing to serve and going AWOL were far less honorable than either of those alternatives, but not, perhaps, dishonorable. By coming here I could pretend for many years that my refusal to serve was an act of courage and conviction. Now I think that it was simply the best of the bad solutions; now I try to put the best face on it—A did not die in Vietnam, and I killed no one there.

On the way to the airport, I thought of trading your story about Tyrone for one of my own, about how Magellan, pursued by the Spanish Armada, led his own fleet into the Horse Latitudes because he knew that no sailor in his right mind would deliberately veer off into that vast water-desert barren of wind, and so he escaped from the Armada, whose captains never thought to look there. But in the meantime, he won the contempt and wrath of the captains and crew of every vessel under his command. I intended to leave you that to chew on for a few years; time robbed me of a chance to tell it, and, much more importantly, it happened that the memory of your fleeing the scene at Garner State Park rushed back to me as your plane lifted off the runway at Regina, and my arm flew up in a reflex to call you back to remind you of it.

Sheets of water from the morning's rain, still as ice to the eye, spread across the runway after your plane was a tiny segment of line in a darkening sky, and I stood at the wire with that memory burning like a vision to weld my world together. You should have known better than to blame me for my choice, you who would have felt the same, patriot or no. I even suspect you might have gone one better—maybe stopped Spores, reported him. We stood on the river bank with mouths agape and hearts in our throats as the child, breathless and hysterical, screamed, "My Daddy's drowning!" waving madly at the clear expanse of river to our front which was smooth and unbroken but for a few ripples carrying a cluster of bubbles. The child's banshee wail and his dervish dance undid us all, adults and children alike, and everyone began hopping on the pebbly beach as if hot-footed. In all honesty I can't say that "without a second's hesitation" you dived into the water, because your first motion seemed convulsive, like a gigantic, coordinated spasm, then you whirled as though unsure of where to go or as if you expected to see someone official go whizzing into the water, but no one did, so you kicked off your shoes and shed your trousers and ran into the river in your sock feet, the water surging around your knees, then plunged forward into the deep green pool where the man had disappeared. We waited; after a long, tense pause, you rose for a huge gasp of air, vanished again. Then you brought the man up, dragged him out onto the bank and gave artificial respiration the old way, with him prone and you astraddle his hips, your palms pressing his rib cage. Finally, he coughed up water, came to.

Who was that masked man? We eased away under cover of noisy whoops of relief from the man's family and slipped off to our campsite, stowed away our gear and drove off before anyone could get your name. Perhaps you would've gotten an award; as a kid I read a book about Carnegie medal winners and was thrilled to think that but for your modesty, you'd have been in it, too.

What I saw too late yesterday as our hands broke apart and you were moving toward your plane with your lean American's worried walk was that we are two idealists squinting at one another across a chasm of American history, alike in more than just our myopia; the gap which separates us is not our difference, but, paradoxically, our likeness: you taught me that the drowning should be saved.

C.W. **Smith** has published many short stories and novels, including *Buffalo Nickel*.

A special issue of the *KENYON REVIEW* focusing on African American, Arab and Asian American, Caribbean, Hispanic and Native American writers: new fiction by Beth Brant, Paule Marshall and Reginald McKnight, poems by Martin Espada, Judith Ortiz Cofer, Joy Harjo, Colleen McElroy, and Ray A. Young Bear, essays on Gwendolyn Brooks and Audre Lorde, plus another two dozen distinguished writers. More than a magazine: this is an anthology you'll want to pass on to friends, share with students.

DeColoRes

Available October 30, 1991.
Single copies: $7.00.
Orders of six or more: 40 percent discount.
Subscriptions: 1 yr: $20; 2 yr: $35; 3 yr: $45.
Foreign: Add $5 postage.
Write: Kenyon Review
Kenyon College
Gambier, Ohio 43022-9623

THE JOURNAL

Recent contributors include:

Linda Bierds
Albert Goldbarth
Liza Wieland
John Repp
T.R. Hummer
Janie Fink
Mike White

Cynthia Ozick
Mary Robison
Jane Shore
David Baker
Edward Kleinschmidt
Eric Pankey
Dennis Schmitz

Elizabeth Spires
David Wagoner
Lawrence Raab
M.V. Clayton
Nancy Zafris
Heather McHugh
Carol Potter

Forthcoming (Fall 1991 Issue):

An Interview with Lore Segal
Poetry by Philip Dacey
Our Second Annual Poetry Feature

and much more

The Journal (formerly *The Ohio Journal*) has been in continuous operation since 1973 at the Ohio State University. The Journal is published twice each year and is supported by the Department of English, the Ohio Arts Council, private contributions, and sales. Submissions must be accompanied by a self-addressed stamped envelope. Copies and a small stipend are given as payment upon publication.

Please me a———— year subscription at a cost of $8.00 (1 year); $16.00 (2 years); $24.00 (3 years).

Name ——————————————————————————

Address ——————————————————————————

City/State/Zip ——————————————————————

Make check or money order payable to **The Journal** and return this form to:

Managing Editor
The Journal
The Ohio State University
Department of English
164 West 17th Avenue
Columbus, OH 43210-1370

In addition to publish-
ing the poems of some of
America's finest poets in every
issue, *The Gettysburg Review* has scheduled the
following special features on poetry:

Focusing
*on*Poetry

SUMMER 1991

Paul Mariani's memoir on his first efforts at poetry; Floyd Collins
on Charles Wright; poems by Gerald Stern, William Matthews,
Michael Waters, Alice Jones.

AUTUMN 1991

A special feature on John Berryman, with essays by Philip
Levine, Paul Mariani, and Mark Jarman; Mark Strand's essay on
Parnassus in American poetry.

WINTER 1992

A special feature on Elizabeth Bishop, including a selection of
her high school writings and essays on her work by Thomas
Travisano and George Lensing.

IN THE FUTURE

An interview with and new work by Stanley Kunitz; a selection
of letters exchanged by James Wright and Robert Bly; Don
Colburn on Keats's "Ode to a Nightingale"; Charles Wright on
his newspaper days; Floyd Collins on current books of poetry.

If you are interested in poetry, you should become a subscriber to
The Gettysburg Review immediately. At only $15 per year (add $5 for
foreign addresses), it is an excellent bargain.

Still available is the issue containing our special feature on James
Wright (Winter 1990), including high school poems, a memoir by
E. L. Doctorow, and an essay by Peter Stitt. Only $6, postage-paid.

Gettysburg
The Gettysburg Review

Gettysburg College / Gettysburg, PA 17325

CONGRATULATIONS!!

TO

Abigail Thomas

**Winner of the $1,000 William Peden Prize
in Fiction**

for her story

"A Tooth For Every Child"

which originally appeared in
The Missouri Review
Volume XIII, Number 3

This year's judge was Will Baker

Thanks again to

FIRST NATIONAL BANK

in Columbia
For their generous sponsorship
in funding this prize